Praise for Geoff Dyer's

WHITE SANDS

"Wry and exquisitely observed." —*The Village Voice*

"Brutally honest. . . . When Dyer's insights gain altitude, they are transcendent, reminding us that every square inch of the planet shimmers with the magnetism of its former life and former meaning."
—*The Boston Globe*

"What is the point of anything, really? That's the basis for much, maybe most, of the comedy in this world. And that's the basis for the singularly entertaining oeuvre of the writer Geoff Dyer."
—*San Francisco Chronicle*

"A thinking person's travelogue through territories geographic, cultural, and personal." —*The Austin Chronicle*

"With his customary elegance of thought, [Dyer] sees that our attempts to transcend our situation through travel and art are motivated by our awareness of our final destination."   —*Financial Times*

"In Dyer's critical gonzoism, the fact-fiction question doesn't matter. . . . What he imagines are the whats and the whys beyond fact and fiction. It's what makes his work fascinating."   —*Santa Fe New Mexican*

"Dyer is entitled to be proud of his cerebral equipment . . . of the way it makes unexpected connections, which is what the firing synapses in our head are supposed to do; of its delight in asking bold metaphysical questions . . . and of its tricksy blurring of the borders between fact and fiction, life and art."
—*The Guardian*

"The arrival of a new Geoff Dyer book is an occasion for which I drop everything. . . . He's witty, insightful, casually brilliant, and frequently profound."
—Janet Potter, *The Millions*

"[Dyer] proves that the art of the essay mirrors that of the art of travel—and that he's a master of both. . . . In paragraphs packed as smartly as a carry-on bag that fits snug in the overhead compartment, with sentences so artfully wrought that they may well shift during flight, Dyer exalts in transporting us elsewhere, into landscapes both exotic and intimate."
—*The Post and Courier* (Charleston, SC)

"There is no other writer quite like Dyer. He is wickedly funny, indefatigably brilliant and almost effortlessly compelling."
—*The Buffalo News*

"*White Sands* shows Dyer in full command of his abilities. He is able to meditate upon (or is the right phrase 'riff on'?) the biggest questions as well as or better than anyone in the game."
—*Austin American-Statesman*

GEOFF DYER

WHITE SANDS

A Fellow of the Royal Society of Literature and a member of the American Academy of Arts and Sciences, Geoff Dyer has received the Somerset Maugham Award, the E. M. Forster Award, a Lannan Literary Fellowship, a National Book Critics Circle Award for criticism, and the Windham Campbell Prize for nonfiction. The author of four novels and nine works of nonfiction, Dyer is writer in residence at the University of Southern California and lives in Los Angeles. His books have been translated into twenty-four languages.

www.geoffdyer.com

WHITE SANDS

WHITE SANDS

...

Experiences from the Outside World

GEOFF DYER

Vintage Books
A Division of Penguin Random House LLC
New York

FIRST VINTAGE BOOKS EDITION, MAY 2017

Grateful acknowledgment is made to Alfred Music for permission to
reprint an excerpt from "Riders on the Storm," words and music by
The Doors, copyright © 1971 and renewed by Doors Music Co.
Reprinted by permission of Alfred Music. All rights reserved.

The acknowledgments for previous publications can be found
following the text.

The Library of Congress has catalogued the Pantheon edition as follows:
Dyer, Geoff.
[Essays. Selections]
White sands : experiences from the outside world / Geoff Dyer.
pages ; cm
I. Title.
PR6054.Y43A6 2016   824'.914—dc23   2015030019

Vintage Books Trade Paperback ISBN: 978-1-101-97012-6
eBook ISBN: 978-1-101-97012-6

Book design by M. Kristen Bearse

www.vintagebooks.com

Printed in the United States of America
10 9 8 7 6 5 4 3 2 1

For Rebecca

The point of going somewhere like the Napo River in Ecuador is not to see the most spectacular anything. It is simply to see what is there. We are here on the planet only once, and might as well get a feel for the place.

—Annie Dillard

There remained the inexplicable mass of rock. The legend tried to explain the inexplicable. As it came out of a substratum of truth it had in turn to end in the inexplicable.

—Franz Kafka

Contents

Note

Like my earlier blockbuster, *Yoga for People Who Can't Be Bothered To Do It,* this book is a mixture of fiction and non-fiction. What's the difference? Well, in fiction stuff can be made up or altered. My wife, for example, is called Rebecca whereas in these pages the narrator's wife is called Jessica. So that's it really. You call yourself the narrator and change the names. But Jessica is there in the non-fiction too. The main point is that the book does not demand to be read according to how far from a presumed dividing line—a line separating certain *forms* and the expectations they engender—it is assumed to stand. In this regard 'White Sands' is both the figure at the centre of the carpet and a blank space on the map.

—GD, California, September 2015

WHITE SANDS

1

Next to my primary and junior schools, in the small town where I grew up (Cheltenham, Gloucestershire) was a large recreation park. During term time we played there at lunchtimes; in the summer holidays, we spent whole afternoons playing football. At one corner of the rec was something we called the Hump: a hump of compacted dirt with trees growing out of it—all that was left, presumably, of the land that had been cleared and flattened to form the rec; either that or—unlikely given the size of the trees—a place where some of the detritus from this process had been heaped up. The Hump was the focal point of all games except football and cricket. It was the first place in my personal landscape that had special significance. It was the place we made for during all sorts of games: the fortress to be stormed, the beachhead to be established (all games, back then, were war games). It was more than what it was, more than what it was called. If we had decided to take peyote or set fire to one of our schoolmates, this is where we would have done it.

Where? What? Where?

In the course of changing planes at LAX, in the midst of the double long-haul from London to French Polynesia, where I was travelling to write about Gauguin and the lure of the exotic in commemoration of the centenary of his death, I lost my most important source of information and reference: David Sweetman's biography of the artist. The panic into which I was plunged by this ill-omened, irreparable and inexplicable loss gradually subsided, giving way to a mood of humid resignation that threatened to dampen the entire trip. Robbed of this essential work—and sometimes loss *is* a form of robbery, even when it is purely the fault of the loser—I spent much of my free time in Tahiti trying to make good that loss, writing down what I remembered of Gauguin's life and work from my reading of Sweetman and other art-historical sources.

Gauguin was nothing if not a character, I wrote, but he was an artist first and foremost. His life was every bit as colourful as his paintings, which influenced all the artists who came after him, including the great colourist

Matisse, who was inspired to travel to Tahiti 'to see its light,' to see if the colours in Gauguin's paintings were for real (they were and weren't). Gauguin was born in Paris in 1848 but thought of himself as 'a savage from Peru,' where he had spent his early childhood. The fact that he was a savage did not prevent him becoming a stockbroker with a wife and family he left behind when he went to Tahiti. Part of the reason for going to Tahiti was to get in touch with his savage roots and shuffle off the veneer of civilization while being able to enjoy all the perks of a French protectorate. The name gives away the colonial game: in classic gangster style, the French offered protection in the full knowledge that what the Tahitians needed protection from was the French. Before Gauguin went to Tahiti he lived for a while in Arles with the tormented genius Vincent van Gogh, and they pretty well drove each other nuts, but of the two Gauguin drove Van Gogh more nuts than Van Gogh drove him nuts, but that is not saying much, because Van Gogh was so highly strung he had it in him to go nuts anyway, was partially nuts even before he went totally nuts. The inherently volatile situation of two artists—as immortalised by Kirk Douglas and Anthony Quinn—living in such close proximity was not helped by their always getting loaded on absinthe, and although it took everyone by surprise it was probably no surprise when Van Gogh cut off his ear to spite his face. Another problem was that Gauguin was a real egotist. He really had a big ego and he was always having to prove himself and eventually he decided that the only way to prove himself was to go to

Tahiti to live among savages, of whom he liked to think he was one. He was forty-three when he got there.

La vai taamu noa to outou hatua

'Where do you come from?' asked the immigration official at Papeete. 'Where are you going?' Had he been briefed to ask these questions—the questions posed by Gauguin in his epic painting of 1897, the questions I had come to Tahiti to answer—as part of the centenary celebrations?

When Gauguin waded ashore in 1891, the local women had all gathered round to laugh at this proto-hippie with his Buffalo Bill hat and shoulder-length hair. When I passed through immigration, they were not laughing but smiling sweetly in the humid, pre-dawn darkness, and they welcomed me and the other tourists with necklaces of flowers that smelled as fresh as they had on the first day of creation. It is always nice to be greeted with a necklace of sweet-smelling tropical flowers but, at the same time, there is often something soul-destroying about it. A lovely tradition of welcome had been so thoroughly commodified and packaged that even though the flowers were fresh and wild and lovely they might as well have been plastic. There was also something soul-sapping about the men driving the tour buses, waiting to 'transfer' the tourists to the barbaric luxury of their hotels: built like prop-forwards, biologically programmed to crush the English at rugby, they were reduced to the role of super-polite baggage handlers.

By the time I checked into my deluxe room it was getting light in that prompt tropical way, so I threw open the French windows, stepped out on to the balcony and took in the pristine view. The dream island of Moorea was backdropped against the half-awake sky. It was a magnificent view as long as you didn't turn your head to the right and see the other balconies geometrically gawping and Gurskying out to sea. I was in a huge and luxurious hotel, and even though the view was fantastic the ocean itself seemed manicured, as if it were actually part of an aquatic golf course to which hotel guests enjoyed exclusive access.

Before everything went pear-shaped between them, Gauguin and Van Gogh had a plan to set up 'the Studio of the Tropics' in Tahiti. These days Papeete, the capital, looks like the kind of place Eric Rohmer might have come if he'd decided to make a film in the tropics: a film where nothing happens, set in a place that resembles a small town in France where you would never dream of taking a holiday, which exists primarily in order to make other places seem alluring—especially if you have the misfortune to arrive on a Sunday, when everywhere is shut. There's not much to see anyway, and on Sunday 'not much' becomes nothing. It would have been wonderful to be here at the tail end of the nineteenth century, when Gauguin first arrived—or so we think.

But Gauguin himself arrived too late. By the time he got here it was 'notorious among all the South Sea Islands as the one most wretchedly debased by "Civilization"': an emblem, I remembered some art historian writing, 'of paradise and of paradise lost.' Only in Gauguin's art would it become paradise regained and reinvented.

When Captain Cook came here it was amazing: a premonition of a picture in a brochure. I went to the spot where Cook—and the *Bounty* and God knows who else—had landed, a place called Venus Point. It is the most famous beach in Tahiti (which, like Bali, has no great beaches even though it is famed for its beaches) and there were a few people sun-bathing and paddling. The sand was black, which made it look like the opposite of paradise, a negative from which an ideal holiday image would subsequently be printed. Or perhaps I was just turned around by the jet lag.

'Are we ten hours behind London or ten hours ahead?' I asked my guide, Joel.

'Behind,' he said. 'New Zealand, on the other hand, is only an hour behind—but it's also a day ahead.' In its intense, near-contradictory concision this was an extremely confusing piece of information to try to compute. That is almost certainly why Joel's next, ostensibly simple remark—'On Sunday this beach is full of people'—struck me as strange, even though, for several seconds, I was not sure why. Then, after an interlude of intense calculation, it came to me: this *was* Sunday—and the beach was almost deserted. It may not have been full of people but it was full of historical significance, and, for a hopeful moment, I had a sense of what it might be like to be a highly regarded species of English novelist: the sort who comes to a place like this and finds inspiration for a sprawling epic, a historical pastiche with a huge cast of characters who contrive to do everything they can to waste the reader's time with what is basically a yarn in which the 'r' might more honestly be printed as a 'w.' Simply by having this thought, it seemed to me, I had effectively written such a novel—all seven hundred pages of it—in a split-second.

From Venus Point we continued our circumnavigation of the island until we came to Teahupoo.

'Do you like surfing?' asked Joel.

'Watching it, yes,' I said.

'That's good, because they hold international surfing championships at this place.'

'Great. You mean they're on now?'

'Almost.' It was a subtle answer, potentially meaning that the championships were either starting tomorrow, had just finished yesterday or even—though this was the least likely option—might actually be in progress by the time we got there. The net result of these permutations was that there were no surfers. Nor for that matter was there any surf, except in so far as the word is contained in the larger term 'surface' (as in 'surface unbroken by waves'). The sea was flat, like a watery pancake. I sensed the emergence of a pattern—of thwarted expectations and disappointed hopes—which had first manifested itself in Boston a month previously.

Gauguin's epic painting *Where Do We Come From?*

What Are We? Where Are We Going? is in the Museum of
Fine Arts there, and, by an astonishing bit of serendip-
ity, shortly before flying to Tahiti, I found myself, for
the first time ever, in Boston. I had been wanting to see
this painting for at least ten years and I was going to
see it shortly before following, as the authors of travel
books like to say, 'in the footsteps of' Gauguin to the
South Seas. Although I had done many other things in
those ten years I had also been *waiting* to find myself
in Boston. And now I was there, in Boston, wandering
through the museum, not even seeking out the painting,
hoping just to come across it, to stumble on it as if by
destined accident, as if I were not even *expecting* it to be
there even though I knew it was there. After seeing some
paintings twice (Turner's *Slave Ship,* Degas's motionless
At the Races) and Bierstadt's *Valley of the Yosemite* three
times, I began to suspect that I had trudged through
every room in the exhausting museum, had been walking in my own footsteps for almost an hour, without
even glimpsing the one I had come to see. Eventually I
asked one of the attendants where *Where Do We Come
From?* had gone. He looked up from the strange limbo
of his station: exhausted, bored out of his mind, wanting
nothing more than to take the weight off his feet but,
at the same time, eager to respond to any enquiry even
though he had already heard every question he was ever
going to be asked a thousand times before. The painting
was not on display at the moment, he said. It was being
restored or out on loan, I forget which. Having thanked
him, I trudged away in a state of disappointment so all-

consuming it felt like he had put a curse on me, a curse by which the force of gravity had suddenly increased threefold. The afternoon would be redeemed—the curse and weight of the world lifted—by an encounter with a painting by a painter I'd never heard of, had never seen in reproduction and had somehow missed during the earlier, pre-letdown trudge through the museum's extensive holdings, but at that point, with no redemption in sight, the experience of the missing masterpiece, of the thwarted pilgrimage (which is not at all the same as a wasted journey), made me see that the vast questions posed by Gauguin's painting had to be supplemented with other, more specific ones. Why do we arrive at a museum on the one day of the week—the only day we have free in a given city—when it is shut? On the day after a blockbuster exhibition has finally—after multiple extensions of its initial four-month run—closed? When the painting we want to see is out on loan to a museum in a city visited a year ago, when the featured show was the Paul Klee retrospective already seen in Copenhagen six months previously? An answer of sorts comes in the form of a droll exchange in Volker Schlöndorff's *Voyager*, an adaptation of Max Frisch's novel *Homo Faber,* in which Faber (Sam Shepard) asks an African guy when the Louvre is open. 'As far as I know it's never open,' he replies with the wisdom of magisterial indifference. All of which leads to another, still more perplexing question: what is the difference between seeing something and not seeing it? More specifically, what is the difference between seeing Tahiti and not seeing it, between going to Tahiti and not going? The answer to that, an answer that is actually an answer to an entirely different question, is that it is possible to go to Tahiti without seeing it.

I was able, at least, to get a sense of the *size* of *Where Do We Come From?* at the Gauguin Museum in the Botanical Gardens of Tahiti, where a full-scale copy now hangs. At the very centre of the painting, an androgynous figure reaches up to pluck a fruit from a tree, though exactly what this symbolises is difficult to say, and there are many other symbols as well. Gauguin was a symbolist, which means his art was full of *symbols*. Even the colours are symbolic of something, even though they often seem symbolic of our inability to interpret them adequately. Not everyone has had the patience to try. For D. H. Lawrence, who stopped briefly in Tahiti en route from Australia to San Francisco, Gauguin was 'a bit snivelling, and his mythology is pathetic.' This visual mythology—a magpie fusion of Maori, Javanese and Egyptian, of anything that appealed to his sophisticated idea of the universal primitive—achieved its final and simplest expression in *Where Do We Come From?* According to the most important mythic element in all of this (the myth, that is, of the artist's life), once Gauguin had finished it he tried to kill himself but ended up overdosing or underdosing. When he had come back from the dead, he spent some time contemplating his answers, his answers in the form of questions in the form of a painting. Then, as with almost all the other paintings he'd done, it was rolled up and shipped back to France, leaving him with little evidence of the world he'd created. It is quite possible that some days he woke up and thought to himself, 'Where did that big painting get to?' and then, as he sat on the edge of the bed, scratching his itchy leg, he would remember that he had sent it off and would have to start another one. In the Gauguin Museum there are little photocopies of all these paintings with captions explaining where in the world they have washed up: the Pushkin in Moscow, the Museum of Modern Art in New York, the Musée d'Orsay in Paris, the Courtauld in London. As part of the centenary, however, forty works of art were being temporarily returned to the island. Following Pissarro's bitchy remark that Gauguin 'is always poaching on someone's land, nowadays he's pillaging the savages of Oceania,' it has been fashionable in recent years to see Gauguin as an embodiment of imperialist adventurism. In this light the return of his works can be read as a gesture of reparation, but it would be a mistake to extrapolate from this, to think that there is a groundswell of support in Polynesia for making the islands independent of France. On the contrary, the fear is that France might one day sever its special connection with Polynesia, thereby staunching the flow of funds on which it is utterly dependent.

After the museum we went to Mataiea and Punaauia (now a featureless suburb of Papeete), where Gauguin lived and where some of his most famous works were painted. I suddenly had the idea that yellow might be a symbol for banana, but apart from that my mind was completely blank and I couldn't think myself into

Gauguin's shoes, couldn't see the world through his eyes. As I stood there, however, seeing what he had seen without even coming close to seeing *as* he had seen, I did get an inkling of the attraction of Islam. Impossible—not even *conceivable*—that a Muslim, on making the mandatory, once-in-a-lifetime pilgrimage to Mecca, could be *disappointed*. That is the essential difference between religious and secular pilgrimage: the latter always has the potential to disappoint. In the wake of this realization there swiftly followed another: that my enormous capacity for disappointment was actually an achievement, a victory. The devastating scale and frequency of my disappointment ('I am down, but not yet defeated,' Gauguin snivel-boasted) was proof of how much I still expected and wanted from the world, of what high hopes I still had of it. When I am no longer capable of disappointment the romance will be gone: I may as well be dead.

A Fuaohipa noa i te taime ati

There's no use putting it off any longer. The unaskable question is crying out to be asked. Not 'Where are we going?' but 'What are the women like?' Are they *babes*? No one was more eager to answer this question than Gauguin himself, and the answer, obviously, was yes, they're total babes in a babelicious paradise of unashamed babedom. Many of Gauguin's most famous paintings are of Tahitian babes who were young and sexy and ate fruit and looked like they were always happy to go to bed with a syphilitic old lech whose legs were covered in weeping eczema. Of course, he was also a great artist, but they didn't know this, since at the time he did not have the reputation that he has now, and to see how great an artist he is you have to know something about art, which they didn't, because they hadn't seen any. To them he was just a randy old goat who was always trying to persuade them to get their kit off, which they were happy to do even though the killjoy missionaries who had come to the island before Gauguin and converted people to boring old Christianity had got them to cover up their breasts. The missionaries made them wear something called a Mother Hubbard, which was a shapeless and not very flattering frock, but Gauguin knew that underneath their Mother Hubbards they were, as a famous British ad campaign from the 1980s had it, 'all loveable,' and their melon-ripe breasts were still there, and were no less nice for not being visible to the naked eye until they were undressed. *They* might not have known he was a great artist but Gauguin believed himself to be one, right up there with Manet, whose *Olympia* bugged him in the sense that it goaded him to do a really horny picture of a naked Polynesian woman, ideally one who was only about thirteen, as much a girl as a woman. At first, though, Gauguin didn't do much painting. He just tried to look and understand what was going on in their heads. He read about Maori art and artists and this helped him understand, but he was an artist, and for an artist looking is its own form of understanding. Earlier visitors to Tahiti had noticed the grace and stillness of its inhabitants, but while they interpreted this as torpor or boredom, Gauguin saw 'something indescribably solemn and religious in the rhythm of their poses, in their strange immobility. In eyes that dream, the troubled surface of an unfathomable enigma.' As well as trying to understand what was going on in their heads he was also keen on getting down their pants, and the other colonials took a dim and possibly envious view of this.

That's how it was in Gauguin's day. But what about now? I can give a very good answer to this, because it so happens that while I was there the finalists for Miss Tahiti were all being photographed by the press, in the luxury of my hotel, looking like they'd stepped straight out of a Gauguin painting. So, yes, Tahitian women, they're really beautiful—especially when they're young. Then, almost overnight, they get incredibly fat. It's as if they discover *Fat Is a Feminist Issue* and gobble it up. They don't just read it; they *eat* it. Not to be outdone, the dudes get *even fatter*. It's like some calorific battle of the sexes. The most popular sport here is canoeing, but the thing at which Polynesians really excel is weight-lifting, otherwise known as walking or standing. Every time they heave themselves out of a chair they equal or exceed a previous personal best. And although the canoe is essentially a slim-fitting vessel, in Tahiti it has presumably adapted and evolved—in a word, expanded—to accommodate the area's distinctive twist on Darwinism: the survival of the fattest. The people are huge. They stare at you from the depths of their blubber. It's like they've gone into hibernation within the folds of their own flesh. Part of the reason for this, according to Joel (slim by Tahitian standards, immense by any others), was that Polynesians have the highest per-capita sugar intake in the world. It so happened that as Joel was saying this I was taking my first, tentative sips of a canned drink called South Sea Island Pineapple. Huge letters proclaimed that it was ARTIFICIALLY FLAVOURED, as though the lack of the natural were a major selling point. A closer reading of the can revealed that it had more Es in it than a nightclub on that other island paradise Ibiza. It was also, by some considerable margin, the sweetest drink I had ever tasted: anecdotal confirmation that, as Joel explained, Polynesians were also the world's number two in diabetes and number three in cardiovascular illnesses related to sugar. Joel reeled off these statistics with a kind of appalled pride, as if this ranking in the league-table of sugar-derived illnesses were the source not only of the nation's obesity but also its pre-eminence.

Another claim to fame announced by Joel is that they've got the highest electricity bills in the world. It would be strange if this were not the case, because everything here costs a big fat arm and a leg. Everything is imported from France, and by the time it's made its way around the world it costs a thousand times what it would in Europe. As I sat down for dinner one starlit night, a waitress waddled over to explain the difference between this over-the-water restaurant and another, less glamorously located elsewhere in the hotel.

'This restaurant is gastronomic,' she said.

'Astronomic, more like!' I quipped.

The fact that it was astronomically expensive meant that I ended up like Gauguin, eating 'dry bread with a glass of water, making myself believe it is a beefsteak.' Metaphorically speaking, anyway. I was actually eating mahi-mahi with vanilla sauce, as I did every night of my stay. Mahi-mahi was in season and vanilla is the opposite of money: it grows on trees—but *still* ends up costing a fortune—and tastes like concentrated essence of artificial flavour, flavour for people whose idea of culinary refinement peaked with bubble gum.

The expense didn't just mean that things cost a lot. It meant that my fellow diners and tourists tended to be on the old side, were usually on a cruise, often a tad *square*—and always in couples. I was surrounded by couples, murmuring couples who amused each other over dinner by tossing bits of baguette into the sea, where they were gobbled up by fat fish. The idea of the all-you-can-eat buffet had been extended to the ocean itself. The fish were so domesticated that if they'd had fingers they'd have signed for the meal and charged it to their room. That the ocean had been tamed in this way contributed to an impression that had been building up in the course of my stay, and which I now communicated to another solitary tourist, an optimistic Australian in whose company I had sought solace.

'We are not in Polynesia at all,' I said. 'We are in a casino in Vegas called the Tahiti or the Bounty.'

'But look out there,' he said. 'Look at that amazing sea.'

'You obviously haven't been to Vegas recently,' I said.

We only chatted together for five minutes, but that was enough to make him my closest friend in Tahiti. Where, I asked myself, were the modern primitives of the international party scene, the tattooed savages with their piercings and dreadlocks whose company I enjoy even if I cannot count myself among their number? They were nowhere to be seen, that's where they were. Even when *I* was nowhere to be seen, when I was alone in my room, I felt a bit embarrassed to be here in this once-natural paradise that had to be cosmetically improved and maintained in order to look perfectly natural. Useful, in an entirely useless way, to discover that embarrassment is not only a public emotion or reaction, that it's possible to experience it in private, when no one is looking. If embarrassment became something else when internalised in this way, if it began to transmute itself into any kind of insight or resolve, it would have something going for it. Instead, it lingers like a blush which deepens the more intensely you try to wish it away.

Tei raro ae the hatua poito i to outo parahiraa

Gauguin stayed in Tahiti for two years. Then he went back to Paris. Then he came back to Tahiti, but he didn't like it, because in the time he'd been away it had got all developed and wasn't savage enough for him any longer, so he decided to go somewhere more remote, to Hiva Oa, north-east of Tahiti, in the Marquesas. He didn't actually get there until 1901, and in the meantime he moaned and groaned and complained about everything, but he never lost the sustaining artistic belief that he could turn everything that happened to him to creative advantage. It was in this period that he produced some of his greatest paintings, many of which had Tahitian titles—*Merahi metua no Tehamana, Manao tupapau*—even though his grasp of the language was fairly flimsy and sometimes these titles did not mean quite what they were meant to mean. Things often went badly. Sometimes he found himself on the brink of despair, but always, at the last moment, something turned up to bring him back from the brink or push him over it—but if he did go over it then it turned out that that was a good thing, because going over the brink had a somewhere-over-the-rainbow quality to Gauguin. Not to put too fine a point on it, he was a martyr to his art. One picture was called *Self-Portrait near Golgotha*—his way of saying that although he was in desperate straits he was going to redeem everything in paintings like this one of himself near Golgotha. All of his other paintings he sent back to France, but the Golgotha one he kept by him and took with him to Hiva Oa so he would always have an image of his own suffering to keep him company and cheer him up. There is a moral in this, as there is a moral in almost everything. In this case the moral is that paradise or what we call paradise is often a kind of Golgotha, as exemplified by the experience of the many tourists who each year find their holiday dream turning into a night-mare as they are stranded at Gatwick for several days due to an air-traffic controllers' dispute in Spain. Either that or their luxury villa turns out to be a crumbling pit with plumbing problems. Gauguin didn't care about things like this. He was happy with a basic hut. He didn't crave a deluxe over-water bungalow, though he was perturbed by the increasingly desperate state of his own plumbing, namely his poxy old schlong, which, frankly, no one in their right mind would chow down on unless they were paid a good deal of money and offered a course of high-dosage penicillin.

The flight to Hiva Oa took three hours, and since, in Gauguin's day, you couldn't just hop on a plane and fly anywhere, it must have taken a long time on a boat, because it's a long way and even now people in Tahiti regard Hiva Oa as the back of beyond, so he really did end up a long way from home, so far away that if he'd gone any further he'd have ended up nearer home, the world being round like a melon.

A simple and single law governs life on remote islands: there is nothing to do except go completely to pieces. Gauguin was no exception, and although he continued working, much of his time on Hiva Oa was spent squabbling with priests and judges and generally making a nuisance of himself. He still painted, but the years of his greatest productivity were behind him, and one day he just died, and although a friend of his bit into his scalp to try to bring him back from the dead it was to no avail, because this time he was not coming back.

He had joined the spirits of the dead who look over naked thirteen-year-old girls, as in the infamous painting *Manao tupapau,* in which, he had said, it is difficult to tell whether she is dreaming of the scary spirit or the spirit is dreaming of her, specifically of her ass, of which we enjoy an unimpeded view. But he had also joined the immortal dead, the great artists of the Western world, the choir visible, and he wanted to lie back and enjoy a view of the posthumous fame to which his strange life was no longer an impediment.

Gauguin is buried in the cemetery near the village of Atuona. There's a rock with his name on it, and a tree. It merits a stop of about two minutes, max, and visiting it was pretty much a non-experience. It did nothing for me, possibly because, a few minutes later, I came to another memorial, to someone I had never heard of:

NAOPUA A PUUFAIFIAU, SOLDAT:
MORT POUR LA FRANCE 1914–18

There are memorials like this throughout France, but none of these had expressed so powerfully the scale of a catastrophe that had engulfed not just Europe but the world. To think that someone born here, in one of the most remote places on earth, could have been sucked into the First World War: Gauguin's movement was centrifugal, from the centre to the edge, but it was counter-balanced by this opposite, centripetal movement compelling someone from the fringes of the world to the epicentre of history. From that moment on it would be impossible, even in paradise, to live in a way that was untouched by history. Working backwards from this, we can deduce that our (historically constructed) idea of paradise is, precisely, a place untouched by history.

After visiting the grave, I was scheduled to spend an hour at the Cultural Centre, which is a facsimile of the house Gauguin built for himself. There was one slight problem: it did not exist. Effectively, I was shown the place where the Cultural Centre was going to be (i.e., a building site). As such it was almost indistinguishable from building sites the world over, but they had begun work on reproducing the carved door-frame that Gauguin made over the threshold of his 'Maison du Jouir': 'Soyez Amoureuses et Vous Serez Heureuses.'

The climax of that day's tour came with the chance to see objects found in Gauguin's well. Actually, that is to put it too grandly. I should say remains or fragments of objects: some broken bottles, bits of crockery, jars, a syringe, ampoules of morphine and clumps of congealed paint. It was, on the one hand, just a load of old junk. On the other hand, it was still a load of old junk, but no more persuasive exhibition has ever been mounted to demonstrate the status of art as religion, the artist as secular martyr. We were pilgrims and these were the relics, invested with all the majesty of Christ's sandals or whatever it is they have in Lourdes. And this secular veneration does at least have the benefit of honesty and scepticism. As the curator explained: although they were found in Gauguin's well, 'we can't certify that they were Gauguin's, but it's quite possible they were.'

. . .

Because Hiva Oa was not beautiful in the way I had expected, it took me a while to see that it was beautiful at all. The island looked both tropical and non-tropical and it seemed that every kind of tree grew here. This was a result not just of the fecundity of the soil but of the long history of trade and exchange. Joel had explained to us that Cook or Bligh (of *Mutiny on the Bounty* fame) had brought the pineapple to Tahiti from somewhere else—Hawaii, I think—and taken away the breadfruit or something like that, but I could not remember the exact details and so was unsure whether the grapefruit was indigenous or imported. Either way, as I was taken on a march through jungle which seemed, in places, more like Sherwood Forest than the lush tropical paradise of Rousseau (Le Douanier), the grapefruit and every other variety of fruit and flower seemed happy to have made a home here. In places the island was lush, in others stark and jagged, cloud-shrouded and desolate. This, together with the cosmopolitan mix of vegetation, meant that it kept looking like somewhere else, mainly like Switzerland in the grips of a record-breaking heat wave. This was not what I had expected at all. I had been expecting to meet local artists who continued a tradition initiated by Gauguin but soon came to see that the real art of the Marquesas, and of Polynesia generally, was tattooing. Everyone here has tattoos of breathtaking geometrical precision, density and intricacy. There was a time when a tattoo was like a bodily

CV conveying all sorts of data: who your mum and dad were, the names of your ancestors, what your trade was (warrior, nobleman), what grade A-levels you got and even, possibly, what you had for lunch last Thursday. The tattoos were the Polynesian way of answering the questions 'Where do we come from?' and 'Where are we going?,' the very questions that religions either answer or—to those of a Nietzschean bent—are designed to stop you answering.

The missionaries buried the pre-Christian, polytheistic religion of Polynesia (and, for a time, put a stop to tattooing) but it is possible to visit some recently excavated sacred sites. The most impressive of these is at Iipona on Hiva Oa, where there are five monumental sculptures or *tiki*.

I was not that keen on going, for several reasons. Instead of recovering from jet lag, I was sleeping less and less every night. I didn't just have jet lag; I had jet-lag lag. I had also developed a terrible heat rash, which was tormenting me every bit as much as Gauguin's eczema, and all I could think about was the non-availability of soothing ointment.

A few days earlier, before the rash really got going, we had visited another archaeological site, which, in its small-scale way, was a monumental disappointment. There were just a few blackened stones that the guide sought to render interesting by nattering on about human sacrifice and cannibalism while I stood there, both not listening and looking like I was listening.

It was a short-lived relief to go from here to another

site—at Taaoa, near Atuona—where the *tiki*'s power had been denuded to almost nothing: a round rock as big as a beach ball on which the residue of a human face—slits for eyes and mouth, the merest hint of a nose—could just about be seen. Aesthetically it was on a par with Wilson, the volleyball with whom Tom Hanks develops such an intense relationship in *Cast Away*. As Hanks ekes out his existence, the longing for *something* in which one can invest belief and hope is shown to be almost as basic as the need for shelter and warmth. The thing—in this case a Wilson volleyball—responds in kind, taking on the magical quality of those hopes. Taaoa, though, was a place that showed how, over time, those beliefs can wane and even a god can have to settle for eking out an existence in a carved bit of rock.

That left just Iipona, the last site on what was turning into an itinerary so wretched that I was bracing myself for some climactic letdown, for disappointment of such purity that I would not even realize it was being experienced: there would be so little at this site, I'd think we were still on our way to it even after we had got there. Such fears proved entirely unfounded.

The jungle had been cleared, the air swarmed with mosquitoes and, as soon as we approached, I felt the gravitational force of the place. I mean that literally. The main *tiki*—the largest in Polynesia—is squat, rounded, strong. There is an unmistakable power here. Even the leaves are conscious of it, can feel it, are part of it. At some level this came as no surprise. There *had* to be something here, lurking or buried in the midst of the island: it was inconceivable that a place like this would not have generated some kind of belief in itself that could be felt—if not understood—by the stranger or visitor.

The denuded features of the round face were thick with moss, emphasising that this stone had no intention of budging, let alone rolling. You need know nothing of the beliefs it incarnates to sense that this is the most earth-bound of gods: as rooted to the spot as a Bulgarian weight-lifter about to attempt a record-breaking clean and jerk, or—going back to an earlier comparison—a Tahitian who has decided never to vacate his seat. This was a Larkin-god: the god of staying put, of not moving. I wanted to stay put, or at least remain longer than the guide had anticipated, to give this god his due and bask in the simplest of emotions (though it is more than that): I was glad I came.

The following day I made another significant discovery as I walked from the hotel down to Atuona, where I hoped to check my e-mail and buy ointment to reduce the torment of my heat rash, which was, if anything, even more tormenting than it had been the previous day. This was the village football pitch. Beyond the touch line, on either side of the pitch, was a mixture of deciduous trees of varied origin (no crowd segregation here). The other end—standing room only—was the preserve of tall palms, swaying together. You'll never walk alone, they seemed to be saying—or, more accurately, you'll never *even* walk, for these were fair-weather fans who only attended home games. Every now and again the wind sent a Mexican wave through the stadium of trees. The pitch was nibbled short, the goal mouths worn out. There were no players, just a dog dribbling (saliva), warming up on the touch line.

A hundred years from now (or a thousand, let's say, to be on the safe side), after it had been overgrown with jungle and then rediscovered by some intrepid archae-ologist and the engulfing vegetation hacked back, this place would have something of the aura of Iipona or, for that matter, of many other places of apparently aban-doned meaning. Assume that only a scanty knowledge of football—the odd picture of Diego Maradona and a few random results (Brazil 2–England 1) rendered meaningless by depth of perspective and the lack of context—had survived that long interlude of neglect and vegetative concealment. The place would *still* have some-thing special about it, if for no other reason than that it was somewhere with no utilitarian function (like grow-ing food or providing shelter), a place that had been set aside, enclosed within its own specific and, some would say, sacred purpose. This is what we would feel, and we would not be wrong if we deduced that the rectangular shapes at either end, the goals, were altars at which peo-ple worshipped and in whose names heroic sacrifices had been made: vestiges of a certain delirium, of a strange and simple faith. You would sense that this was a site of celebration and sorrow, both of which, ultimately, would give way to an all-engulfing sense of futility; that it was a place devoted to a practice with its own rules, which

were at once arbitrary and the generators of meaning, a
set of rules without which this place would not even be a
place. I imagined this future, with the nets gone and the
lines barely noticeable, and immediately realized that it
already looked as it might in this imagined future—and
this in turn made me realize something which should
have been obvious all along: that much geographical
travel is actually a form of time travel, and that I was, to
all intents and purposes, a visitor from a thousand years
hence, come back to puzzle over the significance of this
place.

I sat behind the nearest goal so that it framed the
one at the far end of the pitch. There is always something pleasing about this view of the goal within a goal,
whereby the goal (the far one) becomes a substitute for
the thing (the ball) you are normally trying to force into
it. As I sat there, looking at the goal within a goal, I
thought of the album *Playing* by Don Cherry, Charlie
Haden, Dewey Redman and Ed Blackwell. Like many
ECM records this one has a striking cover: a photograph
of an empty goal post, very white, backed by a wall of
dark green trees (almost a forest). In front of the goal is
the lighter green of the pitch, the lines of which—six-
yard box, penalty area—are impossible to see. Like this
the goal becomes something tangibly abstract, and the
pitch almost a meadow.

I knew all the musicians on the album—that's why
I'd bought it—but knew nothing about the person who
took the cover photograph. He was credited on the back
cover, but I paid it no mind, and the name, in any case,

would have meant nothing to me back then. It was only years later that I came properly to appreciate the identity of the photographer. I was looking through *Kodachrome* by Luigi Ghirri and there it was: the same picture, but as often happens in such circumstances, slightly different. The forest on the album cover had lost some detail, its implied depth, and the grass was somewhat yellowed, drier-looking, either because of faulty reproduction or because, over the years, my copy of the album had faded. The biggest change, however, was simultaneously subtler and clearer, and it was what might be called Ghirri-esque.

Like many Ghirri pictures, this one is quietly but rigorously self-enclosed. The frame within the frame—the frame of the goal posts—concentrates our attention absolutely within the frame of the image (which on *Play-*

ing had been framed again by the white background of the album cover). In the picture there is no narrative to suggest what might be going on either beyond the spatial frame or beyond the moment depicted, because—and this is often the case with Ghirri—there is absolutely nothing going on within it, no hint of movement. This is what a still from a dream might look like. Each picture is pellucid and infinitely mysterious, contains almost no incentive to move on, to turn the page and look at another. We are content to look and wait, to attend. The experience might, in this context, best be described as 'Staying'—which is what I was happy to do, looking at the goal within the goal.

Under the spell of this image of recessive teleology— the goal within the goal—I saw that the intended purpose of coming to Hiva Oa (a Gauguin pilgrimage) was framed not by the lack of a larger goal but by a larger lack of goals, by an all-engulfing purposelessness. This larger lack did not mean, however, that there was no larger perspective. Such a perspective was provided by the empty pitch, whose goal was to show that everything that happened here—the human triumphs and trage- dies, the manly victories and defeats—was lent meaning only as a result of its own continued *non*-human exis- tence. That's to be expected—but the pitch also induced a vision of its own demise, when it would no longer be here, when it would be indistinguishable from the vegetation that would engulf it: the long interlude of forgotten-ness that is a precondition for eventual redis- covery and reclamation. The pitch was like a forgotten photograph depicting the moment when it is remembered and rediscovered.

Uputa

Gauguin's decision to go to the Marquesas is in keeping with the psycho-pathology of island life. 'Polynesia' translates as 'many islands,' all of which you wish you were on instead of the one you actually are on. En route to Hiva Oa we had flown over any number of paradisiacal islands and atolls. In the course of my time here I had become aware of still more islands and atolls, each of which sounded more idyllic—with finer beaches, surrounded by sea more turquoise—than every other. As I studied the guide books and brochures I began to develop a profound resentment against Gauguin, that he had come to Hiva Oa and not to Bora-Bora or Raiatea. I phoned Tahiti Tourism (who had underwritten part of my trip) and pointed out that Gauguin had actually spent a little time on Bora-Bora, but the patient lady with whom I spoke did not feel that this justified changing my itinerary. Well, how about Huahine, I said? But Gauguin did not go there, she said, sounding slightly less patient. Yes, I explained patiently, but perhaps places like this have the appeal *now* that Tahiti did back then. Perhaps, I said, if Gauguin had been alive now he would have gone to Taha'a Noho Ra'a and stayed in an overwater bungalow at the Pearl Beach Resort and Spa as a way of reconciling the savage part of his own nature with the contemporary need for boutique luxury. In the humid heat none of this cut any ice, and it soon became apparent that the question 'Where are we going?' was turning into its vexed opposite, 'Where are we *not* going?'—to which the answer was: all the places I really wanted to go. Other people thought Hiva Oa was paradise, but if this was the case then it was a paradise from which I was becoming impatient to be expelled. With this in mind it seemed certain that the apple in Eden grew on the tree of knowledge of *elsewhere.* Up until that point Adam and Eve were happy where they were. Then they ate the apple and it was slightly *disappointing* to them, and they started to wonder if maybe there were other kinds of apples elsewhere, if there were crunchier and crisper and sweeter apples to be had from somewhere else. They began to think that there might be a funner place, where the food was better. They even began to suspect that *paradise itself* might be somewhere else. And not only that: they began to think that there might be some commercial potential in this knowledge, that it might be possible to make a living importing and exporting these apples and marketing paradise as a *destination.* From there, to keep the history of the world as brief as possible, it is only a small step to package cruises and supermarkets stocking the full spectrum of exotic fruit.

Increasingly, the question on my mind in Hiva Oa was 'When can I leave?' I had exhausted everything the island had to offer, was counting the days to my departure. There was talk of a daytrip to a place where Gauguin's grandson or great-grandson lived. The idea was to have lunch or at least take tea or coffee with him, but it turned out that he doesn't like foreigners and did not want to meet me. Which was fine by me, because I have some dislikes of my own and near the top of that extensive list are the sons, daughters or grandsons and granddaughters of famous parents who consider themselves special by virtue of having been born. Within that general category of detestation I reserve special contempt for those sons and daughters who, while claiming special status from the strength of their lineage, also lament the inhibiting weight of expectation bearing down on them because one or both parents achieved such renown that the pressure on the descendants to do something condemns them to doing nothing, to a life of endless weakness. So fuck you, motherfucker.

In lieu of tea or lunch with Gauguin's heir, I joined some other tourists for a boat trip to a nearby island. The mini-van taking us to the boat was late, but this did not matter because, when we got to the port, the boat was not ready to sail. That was the thing about Hiva Oa: the huge wait to leave contained within it other little pockets of waiting, so that one was caught in an endless hierarchy of waiting. I was always waiting for the next bit of waiting, climaxing with the final day's waiting, in which I would wait to be transferred to the airport, where I would wait for the plane taking me back to Tahiti before the wait for the enormous airborne wait of the flight back to L.A. (more waiting) and on to London itself. In a sense *that* is what we are here for: to wait. In Tahitian terms, *to put on wait*. While waiting, however, one necessarily ponders other questions, questions that don't go away irrespective of how long one waits: the *tiki* questions, the questions *that stay put*, the same questions, according to Harrison Ford's voice-over in the climactic scene of *Blade Runner,* that the replicant Rutger Hauer wanted answered, 'the same answers the rest of us want. Where did I come from? Where am I going? How long have I got?' But the answers to those big questions turn out be small, or at least have to be itemised in detail if they are to have any chance of doing justice to the big questions. We are here to accrue unredeemable air miles and tier points, to try to be upgraded on aeroplanes and in hotels whenever possible, to try to alter our itineraries to include Bora-Bora and Huahine and to wish that the Internet connections were faster and more reliable. We are here to suffer terrible disorientation and jet lag and to be plagued constantly by the desire to be somewhere else, either somewhere else in French Polynesia or, ideally, somewhere else altogether, preferably nearer home. We are here to wish we had brought different books to read and to wonder what happened to our biography of Gauguin. We are here to wish the food was better and to be afflicted by the torment of heat rash and to wish that we had brought some calamine lotion to lessen that torment. We are here to buy presents for our loved ones and then to spend long hours constructing excuses as to why this was impossible because everything in Tahiti is so expensive and there's nothing worth buying anyway.

We are here to be bored rigid and then to wonder how it was possible to be so bored. We are here to wait at Hiva Oa Airport in the drenching humidity and to feel definitively what we have felt before, albeit only fleetingly: that we *are* glad we came even though we spent so much of our time wishing we hadn't. We are here to make sure our seatbelts are securely fastened, our tray tables stowed and our seats are in the upright position before take-off and landing. We are here to go somewhere else.

2

The first area of wilderness to which I had independent access—I went there with my friends, without my parents— was Leckhampton Hill, just outside Cheltenham. A sign warning 'Beware of Adders' emphasised that you had left the safety of the town behind, while imparting a hint of Eden to the untamed outdoors. If you walked here you always came to the Devil's Chimney: a vertical promontory of sandstone rock. I'm not sure whether its origins were natural (a pillar of hard rock left behind when the softer surrounding rock was eroded?) or man-made (the lone residue of what had once been a quarry?). Either way, at some point in its existence it acquired this locally mythic name.

My uncle Daryl and his brother Paul climbed the Devil's Chimney in their teens, in 1958. There is a photograph of them both, bare-chested, perched on top of it like Hillary and Tenzing on the roof of the world. Climbing up must have been difficult, but not nearly as difficult and dangerous as clambering down.

The Devil's Chimney: the place my uncle had climbed. It

was a landmark: a place of mysterious origin where something remarkable and risky had been achieved. It is still there today but is now cordoned off to prevent anyone trying to emulate Daryl's precocious feat.

Forbidden City

On the morning of my visit to the Forbidden City, my last day in China, I woke exhausted, as I had every day of my trip. First, in Shanghai, because of jet lag and the excitement of being in China, then—as the evenings got later, the drinks drunk more numerous, and the morning commitments earlier—from not having enough time to sleep; finally, in Beijing, from a potent combination of all of the above known as lag-induced insomnia.

There was no time for breakfast. There was never time for breakfast. Min was waiting in reception, pre-punctual as always, never tired, always smiling and happy—but with an air of harriedness beneath that smile as she asked if I'd slept well.

'Wonderfully,' I said. It's the easiest thing to do when you've slept terribly: say whatever requires least effort or explanation. We shook hands—we had somehow got stuck at the pre-embrace stage of our relationship—and stepped outside. It was boiling already, at eight in the morning. The driver was standing by the car in a white shirt, his hair slicked back, smoking. I couldn't remember his name. Actually, it wasn't the name but the face that was causing me trouble: the driver's name was Feng, I knew that, but this was not Feng, surely. So, whereas yesterday I'd said, 'Hello, Feng,' today I just said, 'Hi there,' conscious that if this was Feng then he might be offended by the downgrading to anonymity. Was that why he wasn't smiling? No, no, it couldn't be Feng. . . . That was the thing about being so tired, you forgot things you should have remembered—things like people's faces—and then whirred away worrying about them, exhausting yourself still further.

I settled into my seat as the car began its dreadful journey to the Forbidden City. Beijing was a nightmare city, combining the intensity of New York with the vastness of L.A. Was it twenty million people who lived here? A third of the population of Britain in a city that felt about half the size of England. We were on an eight-lane freeway, barely moving. Fine by me: a chance to snatch the first of multiple naps in the course of what Min had already warned would be 'a very tiring day.'

I was jolted awake as the car, having accelerated into an opening, braked and swerved. I'd been asleep for twenty minutes—it was so easy getting to sleep in a moving car in daylight, far easier than in a luxurious bed in a hotel at night. And these twenty-minute naps were incredibly reviving—for about twenty minutes. Min, as usual, was on one of her two phones, sorting out the day's constantly changing schedule. She'd arranged a guide, she said, to show us round the Forbidden City. My heart sank. My heart is prone to sinking, and although few words have the capacity to make it sink as rapidly or deeply as the word 'guide,' plenty of others make it sink like a slow stone: words like 'having to' or 'listen to,' as in having to listen to a guide tell me stuff about the For-bidden City I could read about in a book back home, by which time any desire to do so would have sunk without trace.

We were at the entrance to the Forbidden City. I'd driven past it last night, in a different car, under the Chi-nese moonlight, after a dinner featuring twenty different kinds of tofu, en route to a bar with a view overlooking the moonlit roofs of the Forbidden City. The highlight of the meal had been spare ribs, made of tofu and tasting every bit as meaty as a meat-lover's dream of ribs without the underlying horror of meat. There had even been a shiny bone sticking out of the tofu-meat, made of lotus root. I'd been dreading three things about China: the pollution, the smoking (a subset of pollution) and the food. The air had been clear, I'd encountered hardly any smoking and the food—the tofu—had been like a new frontier in simulation.

I climbed out of the car, walloped right away by the heat even though it was not yet nine. The guide was run-ning late, Min said before hurrying off to buy tickets, so we would meet her inside.

'Great,' I said, hoping the guide would be unable to find us amid the crowds swarming through the gate as though this was the only day of the year entry was not forbidden. Min reappeared with the tickets and we filed into the epic courtyard—already busy, even though we had arrived only moments after tickets went on sale. It was tremendous, this initial view: red walls and golden roofs sagging and boatlike under an ocean of unpolluted sky. We walked into the next courtyard. There were a lot of people here too, but the Forbidden City was the size of Cheltenham, so there was plenty of room for everyone. Jeez, it went on forever, and every bit looked exactly the same as every other bit: courtyards the size of football pitches, cloisters, sloping roofs with rooms beneath them. Doubtless the guide would explain how all these bits were not really alike, how each part had its own particular and tedious function that distinguished it from all the others. All the more reason to enjoy it now in a state of fully achieved ignorance, without the effort of appearing to listen as the guide gnawed away at the experience with unwanted knowledge and unasked-for expertise.

Min was in increasingly frequent communication with this guide, then was suddenly waving to her. And there she was, waving back. Her hair, inky-slinky black, came down to her shoulders. Her complexion was darker than many of the visitors to the Forbidden City, who were so pale they sheltered from the scorch beneath glowing pink umbrellas. She had a big smile, was wearing a long dress, pale green, sleeveless. She walked towards Min, took off her sunglasses and embraced her. She was holding her sunglasses in one hand behind Min's back. Her eyes were brown, round but subtly elongated. I liked her confidence (it made me feel confident, even if it also made me wish, simultaneously, that I'd not worn shorts), the way she stood, wearing sandals with a slight heel. Her toenails were painted dark blue. Her name was Li. We shook hands. A bare arm was extended, and then her eyes disappeared again behind her sunglasses. The thirty seconds since she'd waved were more than enough to reverse all previous ideas about a guide. A guide was an excellent idea. What could be better than having the history of this fascinating place explained at length, in all its intricate detail? Without the application of some kind of knowledge I would not be seeing the place at all, just drifting through it in a mist of ignorance and unachieved indifference.

The three of us stepped out of the hot shade and into the blazing sun of the courtyard or whatever it should properly be called—Li didn't elucidate. I watched her flash into the sunlight and we continued our tour of the Forbidden City. We peered inside a couple of dusty-looking rooms, but there was nothing to see except exhausted beds and depressed chairs. Not that it mattered: the interiors were irrelevant compared with the red-and-gold exteriors, all on an unimaginable scale—the full extent of which Li seemed in no hurry to divulge. She seemed so reluctant to begin her spiel that I prompted her with a few questions, the answers to which I would normally have dreaded.

'I'm afraid I don't really know anything about the Forbidden City,' she said.

'I thought you were a guide.'

'No, I'm just a friend of Min's. She asked me to come.'

Mornings like this prove that you really have to be

mad ever to kill yourself. Contemplate it by all means, but never commit to it. Life can improve beyond recognition in the space of a moment. On this occasion life had been pretty good anyway and then it had got better still—and got still better when Li said, 'If you want me to be a guide, I can try.'

'Yes, go on. Give it a shot.'

'Well, let me see. There was a time when the emperor's wives all lived here. They couldn't leave. All they could do was walk around. It must have been so boring. Except everyone was always plotting. Not necessarily to get rid of the emperor or one of the other wives, partly just to kill the time. It was intriguing all the time.'

'Your English is fantastic. Intriguing.'

'Thank you.'

'Where did you learn?'

'Here in Beijing. And then in London. I lived in Camden Town. It was . . . ' In spite of her language skills she paused, searching for a less bland variant of *very nice*. 'Well, it was rather horrible, if I may say.' Ah, she'd been worried about offending me.

'What else? Not about Camden, which is famously vile. This place—the wives, the emperor.'

'All they wanted, the wives, was for the emperor to love them.' She said it with such conviction it seemed as if she were not just telling their story; she was petitioning on their behalf.

'And what did he want?'

'More wives,' she said. 'And to get away from the wives he had.' Was Li married? I glanced at her long, ringless fingers. Looking at her extremities, her fingers and toes, I felt less exposed than at all points in between.

Always concerned about my welfare, Min had gone to buy bottles of water, which glinted in the sun as she carried them over. We all retreated into the shade and continued our stroll, gulping water. I watched Li drink: her hand, the bottle, the water, her lips. We sat on a low wall, looking at the worn grass and cobbles of the courtyard.

'To our left,' said Li, 'you will admire the Hall of Mental Cultivation.' We were in the shade, looking at a sign in the sunlight that said 'Hall of Mental Cultivation.'

'You're too modest,' I said. 'You actually know a great deal about this place. All sorts of arcane stuff that the foreign tourist could never work out for himself.' I was very taken with the Hall of Mental Cultivation. It sounded so much more relaxing than sitting in the Bodleian and ordering up dreary books from the stacks, but maybe it was more demanding—and enlightening too. Perhaps, in a way that seemed vaguely Chinese, the Hall of Mental Cultivation *was* the sign showing the way to the Hall of Mental Cultivation. I was happy with this thought, a sign that I was already cultivating my mental faculties, which were becoming concentrated, almost entirely, on Li. Conscious of this, of how rude it might appear, I tore my gaze from her and chatted with Min until she had to take a call updating the afternoon's schedule.

The three of us walked in the direction indicated by the sign, came to an empty room that was just an empty room like all the others, though the emptiness it contained must have been qualitatively different to that found in the uncultivated elsewhere.

We could only be out in the sun for five minutes at a time. It was roasting, the sky a burned blue. A month earlier, walking through London at ten on a cloudy evening, I'd been told that this was what Beijing looked like at midday: nearly dark with pollution. I'd had a cough at the time and that was also a foretaste of Beijing, apparently; it was impossible to go there without succumbing to a serious throat or lung infection. I told Li what I'd heard: that the pollution was so bad you could see it falling from the sky.

'A few years ago we broke the record for air pollution. We didn't only beat record. The machine for measuring broke also. The pollution was so bad the measure—how you say?'

'Gauge?'

'Yes, the gauge could not measure it.'

'It was off the scale.'

'It was terrible. . . . '

Li took out her phone; she had an air-quality app which confirmed that the air today was, relatively speaking, mountain-clear. Expats I'd met all had these air-quality apps too, but the source for their measurements was the U.S. Embassy, whose figures were always twice that of the official Chinese figures. None of that mattered as we walked through the magically unpolluted but still-roasting air of the Forbidden City, which easily lived up to its billing as one of the wonders of the world. If it *was* one of the wonders of the world; I could remem-

ber only two others, the Hanging Gardens of Baby-
lon and the pyramids. Did the Hanging Gardens even
exist anymore? Had they ever—in the solipsistic sense
of within my lifetime—or had they only been included
as a mythic leftover from the vanished past? These days
the whole idea of Seven stately Wonders had an elegiac
feel: a standard of excellence rendered obsolete by bucket
lists of a hundred things to do before you die, whether
bungee-jumping over the Zambezi or losing your mind
on mushrooms at a full-moon party at Ko Pha Ngan,
neither of which I'd done, both of which were on my list
of things to avoid before giving the bucket its final kick.

We paused in the corner of yet another square, heading to the Imperial Garden. Li was drinking water. As
she raised the bottle to her lips I could see her armpit,
hairless and unsweating. And a small scar at the edge of
her mouth. It could only be seen when she was in sunlight, when that side of her face was turned to the sun.
Min suggested she take a picture of the two of us, of Li
and me together. I put my arm around Li's shoulder but
didn't dare touch her bare skin. When I looked at it later
the photo seemed marred by my hand, bunched in a fist
like a potato.

'You look so handsome,' said Min, glancing at the
image on the back of the camera, taking another. She
was always saying things like that. A surprising number
of her colleagues from the publishing house said the
same thing, in fact, and I was not at all displeased to
hear these nice things. It might even have been true in
a way. The friend who'd warned me about the pollution

had also warned—in the sense of reassured—that Chinese women found white middle-aged men attractive. Was this true or was it a kind of mirror projection of the yellow fever to which Western men succumbed? Either way, the constant flow of charm from Min and her colleagues, combined with how young everyone looked, lulled me into behaving like an attractive young man. I became so at home with this new self-image that, on Nanjing Road in Shanghai, I'd glared with disdain at a middle-aged Westerner coming towards me with an expression of barely concealed contempt. The mirrored window had been polished to such a shine that the awful truth took another second to reveal itself. I had bumped, almost literally, into my own reflection: the self as pink-faced other. Right now, flattered by Min and having my picture taken with Li, that was a faded, possibly false memory. And Min's capacity to make me feel better about myself and the world knew no bounds. It was too hot for her, she said. She had to make arrangements with the driver; she would meet us outside in half an hour.

'Really? Are you sure?' I said, glad that I had my sunglasses on in case any sign of excitement manifested itself in my face, my tanned and rugged face. Min was sure; she would see us in twenty minutes. She began walking back the way we had come, sticking to the borders of shade. So now it was just the two of us, just me and Li and about a million other visitors, strolling through the Forbidden City. It would have been the most natural thing in the world—and entirely impossible—to take her by the hand, to stroll hand in hand through the

Forbidden City. It would have been nice to wander for the rest of the day, like Adam and Eve in some crowded paradise of the ancient East, until we came to a distant and shaded spot, to have found this place and sat down where no one could see us, away from the prying eyes of wives and visitors, far from intrigue and at its exact centre. She drank from the sun-scalded bottle until it was empty. The repeated word in all this—'until'—bounced and echoed in my head until it was time to leave, to go and meet Min.

We walked out of the gate, found Min, the car and the driver, who was standing there in a white shirt, his hair slicked back, smoking—but smiling, pleased to see me. This *was* Feng, for sure.

'Different car to this morning, same model,' Min explained. 'And different driver. Same driver as yesterday.' She got in the back behind him, behind Feng. Li sat in the front, I sat in the back with Min, behind Li. We drove for ten minutes until, at some unknown place in the city, Feng pulled over so that Li could get out. I clambered out too, surrounded by the heat-roar of traffic. She had to go back to her work. It was fine to shake hands and to kiss her goodbye, on the cheek, on the side of the face with the small scar. We talked about our respective evenings. She gave me her bilingual card, holding it with both hands.

'I'm afraid I don't have a card,' I said. 'But perhaps we will be able to meet later tonight, after dinner. I hope we can.'

I'd said it casually but had never said anything more

heartfelt. In my teens the prospect of going on a date with a girl I'd just met crushed my chest with excitement. Was that the physiognomic etymology of *having a crush* on someone?

She also hoped we could meet later, she said before turning away, leaving. I tucked her card carefully into one of the many pockets of my shorts and clambered back into the cool car. By the time I looked out of the window she had already disappeared into the crowd. The car eased back into the relentless traffic. Chatting with Min, I touched the sharp edges of the card, resisting the urge to take it out and pore over the amazing information printed on it: her phone number, her e-mail address. There was a time—it seemed to last from my mid-teens to early forties—when it was so difficult to get women's phone numbers that a night out was considered a major success if you came home with a single number scrawled indecipherably on a piece of paper: a number you called with much trepidation, unsure if a father or, later, a boyfriend might answer. On reflection, Li had been a little reserved about handing over her phone number; in Asia it was usually the first thing anyone did.

The afternoon was, as Min had promised, exhausting: a succession of interviews which involved saying the same thing over and over, with less and less conviction, sometimes drifting off in the middle of my shtick and forgetting what I was saying, had said or was planning to say. I'd heard of soldiers being so weary they could sleep while marching, but that option was not available for the weary author being asked about his work, conscious all the time of the problem that, while he talked about his book—a history of improvisation in music, a major theme of which was the necessity of being at home in the moment—or waited for the interpreter to translate the answers, he was always either replaying sequences of Li walking through the Forbidden City, her bare shoulders, her green dress, or looking ahead to the evening, calculating the earliest possible moment they could meet again.

By the time the interviews came to an end I was in a waking coma of non-attention. Min phoned Feng from the lobby of the building. He was stuck in traffic, she said. Not far away in distance but with no chance of getting here for at least an hour. The sidewalks were jammed with people trying to hail taxis, all of which were full, none of which were moving in the dreadful traffic and the terrific heat. It would be quickest, Min said, to take the subway.

'We must improvise!' she said. 'Though it will be very crowded.'

'That's fine,' I said. 'Any half-decent city has crowded subways.'

But none had subways as crowded as Beijing's. Every part of the process—buying tickets, going through barriers and along walkways (the longest, surely, of any subway anywhere in the world)—was exhausting, and every part of the subway system was packed to bursting. Any corridor we had to go down was a solid mass of citizens, from beginning to end. For each of the two changes, we had to queue to get on a train when it came, not with any hope of getting on but with the hope of securing a better position when the train after next pulled in. There was no queue-barging and no pushing and shoving; everyone had adapted to living in crowds and went politely about their tightly packed business.

I was shattered by the time I got back to the hotel, to the room where I'd woken up feeling shattered ten hours earlier, but there was no time to unshatter myself by taking a nap, as I'd banked on doing in the car that was supposed to have met us, before the truly shattering experience of taking the subway back to the hotel. There was time only to shower, change into fresh underwear, a clean blue shirt—the last clean one, kept in reserve— and jeans before meeting Min in reception. We were going to a restaurant to eat Peking duck. This, Min explained, would mark the symbolic end of my visit: the eating of Peking duck in a restaurant in Peking famed for its Peking duck.

It was only a five-minute walk away. The pictures in the elevator showed dozens of the world's leaders and celebrities eating Peking duck, though the restaurant in the pictures didn't necessarily look like the one we stepped into when the elevator doors opened.

There were six of us for dinner, in a private dining room. Qiang, the head of the publishing house, was there, and Wei, whom I hadn't seen for a couple of days. She was wearing jeans and a white T-shirt with something written on it in Chinese characters, and carrying, as always, a pink rucksack made out of some soft and fluffy material. When we'd first met I'd guessed that she was Qiang's daughter, accompanying him during the school holidays. In the rucksack, I assumed, were a few toys or computer games to stop her getting bored—until I passed it to her and found that it weighed a ton. It was crammed with books, a laptop and various electronic accessories. She was twenty-four, the marketing manager. The reason I hadn't seen her for a couple of days was that she'd been taking care of another visiting writer, Jun, from Hong Kong. She introduced us; we shook hands. Jun was exactly my age but, unusually in a part of the world where everyone seemed a decade younger than they were, looked five years older.

Like the Forbidden City, the Peking duck lived up to its considerable reputation, but all the time I was folding slices of duck into the pancakes, adding scallions and other bits and pieces, constantly commenting on its deliciousness, I was conscious of trying to speed things along so that I could meet Li again, even though there was no point in hurrying because she was busy eating dinner herself, not gobbling her food, not fretting and worrying about when we might meet.

I soon had something else to fret about. I'd left my phone at the hotel, in my shorts, and so Min—obliging as ever—called Li and fixed up a rendezvous. It was at a bar, only twenty minutes away, and Jun, Min and Wei were all coming too. Not quite how I had envisaged the rest of the evening panning out, obviously, but perhaps it wasn't a bad idea to dilute my eagerness, to prevent it

acquiring a touch of desperation. We found a taxi immediately; the roads were almost empty. For ten minutes we
sped along, then were obliged to slow to a crawl before
crawling to a halt as the traffic congealed around us. We
were still in the car an hour later, had waited twenty minutes to make a left turn—the lights turned to green for
less than thirty seconds—onto the road the bar was on.
If we'd known this we could have jumped ship, walked
to the bar in five minutes and saved fifteen—a quarter of
an hour. Except, even when we did get out, on the street
itself, the bar was nowhere to be seen. It was a street
full of bars—horrible places, some with pole dancing,
all crowded with young youth, the youthful young—
like a shinier, slightly less ghastly incarnation of Camden Town. Surely she wouldn't have chosen one of *these*
bars. And if she had, then where the fuck was it? Where
was *she*? More time ticked pointlessly away. A minute
was like five minutes. Ten hours from now I'd be on a
flight to London. Then I saw her, waving as she had that
same morning in the Forbidden City, minus the shades.
She was wearing a blue dress, shorter than the one she'd
worn earlier. Darker too, knee-length, but also sleeveless,
revealing the same shoulders and arms. No wonder we
hadn't been able to find the place: she was outside a *nail*
bar. I looked down at her feet, her sandals, her toes, her
blue nails. Min introduced Jun and Wei to Li and we
followed her along a passageway to the side of the nail
bar. We came to a dented grey elevator, large enough to
accommodate a patient on a gurney in an under-funded
hospital, with weary staff and several anxious family

members. The doors squeezed shut; the elevator shuddered upwards until the doors opened again to reveal a dim landing lacking all distinguishing features except some partially erased graffiti. It was an evening when one kind of disappointment followed swiftly on the heels of another, interrupted by surges of hope and renewed expectation. I followed Li up a flight of concrete stairs, the muscles in her calves flexing as she took the steps. But where was she taking us? To a crack den?

No! To a rooftop bar. When we emerged into the hot night, it was like a dream of Ibiza, one of the wonders of the nocturnal world.

'What's it called, this place?' I asked.

'It is the Bar of Mental Cultivation,' she said. 'Did you not see the sign?'

'I'm pretty sure there was no sign. But maybe I was looking for the wrong sort of sign. Like the Dog and Duck.' It was a pub joke, wasted on Li.

The bar was surrounded on three sides by high-rise office buildings, gleaming and new—some so new they were not even finished. On the fourth side the city stretched away forever: neon-topped skyscrapers, the blinking lights of planes. The music was not loud. She had chosen the perfect place, but it was not quite perfect: there was nowhere to sit. Li introduced two friends, both women, who had been here a while, trying without success to secure a table. The best option was for us all to crowd into the psychedelic pod in the middle of the roof, on cushions, but that would have been like sitting inside, not out in the night with the stars overhead. These stars

were nowhere to be seen, there was too much light pollution for that—come to think of it, where had last night's
moon got to?—but the light was not pollution at all,
it was its own kind of magic. We milled around in a
way that was like a standing version of being back in
the car, close to where we wanted to be, but stuck at
a frustrating remove from it. There were a few empty
chairs scattered around, not enough to combine and seat
a party of seven. Then a large group, all male, Chinese
and Western, got up to leave, vacating a large sofa and
some chairs. Li pounced. Once Jun had grabbed two
extra chairs we were in place, all of us together around a
low table—with me seated next to Li on the sofa, without seeming to have done so deliberately.

A waiter took the complicated drinks order: beer,
cocktails, gin, wine. Now that we were settled, with
drinks on the way, everyone was re-introduced. One of
Li's friends turned out to be her sister.

'You don't look at all alike,' I said. Her face was angular, sharp, almost hard.

'She is not real sister,' said Li. 'She is cousin-sister.'
The cousin-sister was a dancer, though she looked too
tall to be a dancer. And she'd just had a baby. The waiter
came back with a tray loaded with glasses, bottles, ice,
drinks. Li had ordered a Singapore Sling ('whatever that
is'); I was drinking beer. Min proposed a toast to me and
Jun. As soon as we had all clinked glasses I offered one
back—'To the Chinese century!'—and we all clinked
again. The beer was only Tsingtao but it was cold, wonderful, tasted OK. For the first time since leaving the

Forbidden City, I was able to give myself entirely to the moment. But if a moment is this perfect there is a need to preserve it, to photograph it. When people are having a good time they take pictures to show and prove they're having a good time. Everyone was taking pictures, not just the people in our group, but all around. What's the point? These pictures never capture the magic of magical evenings, they just show people getting red-eyed drunk and taking pictures of each other, but the act of taking the pictures is part and proof of the moment. It was something I associated with the young, but Jun was at it too. The difference was that he was using a proper camera, not just a phone, and taking considerable care, altering the focus and aperture. At one point he changed the lens in an unobtrusive, unfussy way, still holding his beer, not talking. Then he got up and left the table and walked away, continued photographing at a distance. When he sat back down he passed around the camera so that everyone could see the results.

They were fantastic. I had never been in a situation where something I was experiencing had been caught so perfectly on film. These were pictures of the inside of my head. The photographs were beautiful but, everyone agreed, the best ones were of Li's cousin-sister. The colours were slurred, gorgeous, drenched. In one picture there was a yellow smear of light and, to the right, a string of blurred blue dots stranding her in shadowed clarity. Had Jun known what the result would be? If so, how had he done it?

'He must be in love with her!' I said, answering

my own question. This romantic and technologically ignorant reaction was also a vicarious declaration and attempted deflection of what might have been obvious to everyone. If you were to fall in love with someone, on a rooftop bar in Beijing, this was what it would look like. Or was it just the camera that was in love with the cousin-sister? I'd read that Muhammad Ali, along with his other attributes, had the perfect *face* for a boxer, with rounded features that made him less susceptible to cuts. Li's cousin-sister had the opposite kind of face: angular, sharp-featured. The camera didn't glide or slip from her face in the way that punches slid off Ali's. It clung to her as you hang on someone's every word when you are falling in love with them. The shutter speed, presumably, was however-many-hundredths of a second, but something about her face meant that the camera held it fractionally longer and, in the process, softened it. Her face allowed, even encouraged the camera to do this, to bring her inner life to the surface. She was removed, not quite there. Maybe she was thinking of the child at home? She looked—and again the softened sharpness of her features played a part—*abstracted*. Maybe this was what Jun had noticed, that her face had that special quality or capacity.

I was glad to be able to concentrate on the pictures, to avoid directing my attention completely on Li— especially since, as we had bent forward together to study the camera, our shoulders had touched. They were still touching—my shirt against her bare skin—as we clicked though the images and came to one taken five minutes earlier, showing the two of us sitting where we were now, surrounded by a blue like the blue of oceans seen from space, with the moon above my head. (I glanced around—yes, there it was, peeking out from behind a building.) At first the picture was a little confusing: Li was twisted round, her head was hidden behind me so that only her left shoulder could be seen. I had leaned forward while she reached behind me to retrieve her bag from the end of the sofa, so it looked like she was jokily hiding from the prying camera. There was a subtle intimacy about the interplay of bodies and limbs, what was revealed and hidden. Again, was this an accident— something the camera had accidentally caught—or was it something Jun had noticed and quickly captured? Everything was blurred and coloured by the fairy lights: slow yellows, stretched reds. The softness of the night was implied, its heat and promise, and the uncertainty as to whether I was responding to something that existed in a haze of intangible and unspoken signs. That was also there in the photograph as we looked at it, forearms damply touching, certainly.

Li pointed at my face on the screen, clicked to enlarge it.

'Ah, you a-rook rike George Crooney!' she said, eyes wide. She had never 'r'-ed her 'l's like this before. By breaking the spell, she cast me into it more deeply. And she had out-pubbed me too.

Li handed back the camera to Min—having first taken care, I noticed, to click back to an unincriminating wide shot that showed the whole group together. Min passed it to Jun. The waiter came back with another trayful of drinks. More people were arriving, some of whom knew Li's friends. The bar filled up; the music grew louder but not loud enough to cover up the way that time, which had already ticked away pointlessly in the car, was continuing to tick away, more loudly and pointedly by the minute.

Then, everyone agreed, it was time to go. It was two in the morning. My flight was eight hours from now. The bill was paid—by the Chinese; my money was stuffed back into my hand, as it had been every time I'd tried to pay for anything. We stood up and left the roof. The dismal elevator returned us to the still-busy street with its crude lights and lusts. There was much milling around, waiting for taxis, as everyone in the now-expanded group worked out who was going in which direction. Li was by my side. With a little contrivance I could whisper to her, 'Can I come home with you?' or 'Will you come back to my hotel?' It was premature to propose such a thing and, at the same time, almost too late. And even if she said yes, how to navigate the complications of taxi taking, how to avoid the assumed arrangement of sharing a taxi with Min, Jun and Wei? There was, in addition, the gulf between the polite reasonableness of the question—'Can I come home with you?'—and everything the answer to it might allow, all that could become unforbidden. Why was it—what law of the barely possible decreed—that these situations only cropped up on one's last night, so that instead of falling asleep and waking up with her, instead of eating breakfast and spending the day getting to know her, I would get on a plane a few hours later and leave with an even greater sense of regret because, instead of having missed out on all of this totally, we would have experienced just enough to make us realize how much more we had missed out on by not missing out on it entirely? Li was still by my side. I turned towards her, spoke in her ear. Two taxis pulled up, one behind the other. Hours and minutes had ticked by. Doors were opening, goodbyes being said. There were not even minutes left, only seconds before she would turn towards me so that I could kiss her goodbye—or turn towards me and not say goodbye, not turn away.

3

Maybe because of some fluke of geomorphology, certain places in a landscape develop a special quality. A slight indentation becomes moist, a river runs through it. This becomes a fertility site, devoted to the goddess, the earth mother. To mark the place people arrange a few stones in the symbolic shape of a phallus or vagina so that its power is increased, enclosed, harnessed. A childless couple go there and mutter a few pleasantries and, that very night, the wife conceives. News of this miracle spreads. People travel from afar, hoping for a similar result, believing that coming here will bring their shaming sterility to an end. And it works. Up to a point. Then it doesn't. The explanation is obvious: during a period of drought the river has dried up. Lacking any knowledge of meteorology, the people who live nearby, who have by now become dependent on the business generated by pilgrims, ask the priests (also dependent on the pilgrim trade) what to do. They decide that the only way forward is to moisten up the earth goddess with the blood of a few virgins or adolescent males. So they do that, and this previously nice place acquires an atrocious dimension *which, far from cancelling out its sacred status, enhances it. Or maybe they enlarge the simple stone shrine and build something larger, along the lines of Angkor Wat or Salisbury Cathedral. Then, after an invasion or two, everyone forgets what it was for, and the place falls into disuse and ruin. But the accumulated effect of all these comings and goings lingers and seeps down into the foundations; by falling into ruin its primal circuitry is laid bare. Even when there are just a few stones left and no one knows what went on here, the place retains what D. H. Lawrence, in an essay on Taos Pueblo, called a kind of 'nodality.'*

Space in Time

We came to a place that seemed like nothing much: a homesteader's cabin and a windmill, in the middle of a vast nowhere. The windmill must have been turning, because the wind was sprinting across the plateau. The sky was not just clear or blue. It was as if we'd ended up in a future where there was no atmosphere—no *sky*—to insulate earth from cosmos. Scrub extended into the distance, and in that distance were mountains, but even the things that were near were distant. The land was camouflage-coloured, the dust a dryish, dusty brown. The sagebrush was greyish green, as if emerging from a period of drought or hibernation. Near the cabin but still quite distant, almost invisible, were sticks stuck randomly in the ground—quite a lot of them, some in the far distance as opposed to the near distance but none in the very far distance, where we could not have seen them even if they had been there.

There were three bedrooms in the wood cabin. A fire, specifically a pellet-burning stove, was burning, but we did not linger inside. The air was thin, cold, the sun hot on one's face. When the wind subsided, as it did every few minutes, it was still and quiet and warmer. As we walked towards the sticks it became obvious that there were more of them than we'd realized, though it was difficult to say how many, because many were hard to see and some were not see-able at all, and it is probably only in retrospect, once we had understood that their being invisible was part of their function, that we knew they were there.

The sticks, it became evident, once we got close to them, were not sticks but poles: polished steel, shining in the sun. Reflected down the middle of the first one I came to was a long blue smear: me, my reflected self, distorted and elongated almost to nothing. The poles were sharply pointed, roughly three times my height. They were absolutely vertical, two inches in diameter and cold to the touch, inanimate and inorganic. If they had been tall wooden sticks they could have been planted hundreds of thousands of years ago; being stainless steel, they were, obviously, of more recent provenance. Hundreds of years from now they would still gleam like a promise of the future.

We continued walking until there were poles on all sides, surrounding us, but because they were a long way apart—so far apart one could easily forget they were there—it was the opposite of feeling hemmed in, as if by a forest. Still, it was difficult to detect any pattern or order, and unless you were right next to a pole there was nothing much to look at. The most eye-catching objects were the cabin and the windmill. The cabin was low and squat, hugging the ground, determined to stay put in the face of whatever forces—meteorological, economic—might try to persuade it to budge. Our approach was different. We moved away from each other, in different directions. Being here encouraged us to separate, but we all felt this urge and so the urge to be separate was shared, communal. It was seeing the others, realizing how far away they were, that brought home how far into the distance the poles extended.

The sky was still nothing—no cloud, no anything. Perhaps the poles played a part in this. We rely on scenarios and correspondences to make sense of the world. It was very windy. If there had been a flag it would have blown out straight, proud and American, and there was a suggestion of flag because of the abundance of poles and wind, but there were no flags. It wasn't just that there happened not to be any flags. There was an implied absence of flags.

'We're a small number of people in a very large space,' Ethan said, walking to within talking distance. 'The poles make you come back to a single question: what difference do the poles make? Their effect is both slight and absolute.' We were standing side by side, looking into the distance, Western-style, and then we drifted apart again. The wind was strong enough to make the poles quiver, as if shivering from the cold.

At some point everyone convened at the cabin. I was the last man in and could see the other members of our expedition sitting on the wooden porch, in wooden rockers and on wooden benches, drinking champagne, watching me walk towards them. It was the kind of hut you see in Walker Evans's photographs from the 1930s. What had seemed noble but squalid then seemed idyllic now, especially with the champagne and laughter.

'In a way it's the greatest boutique hotel in the world,' said Jessica as I joined them on the porch. She was right. There were none of the things that make a place horrible: damp carpet in the bathrooms, depressing curtains or floral bedspreads. There was just this wooden cabin, shelter in a shelterless world.

As the sun moved though the absent sky the poles sprouted shadows. The tips sparkled as if stars had perched on them. The sun began to drop towards the horizon; the poles became far more clearly defined. Perspective became an issue in that there was none. Or, rather, there were so many competing perspectives that they complicated each other and cancelled each other out. Though still slender, the poles acquired bulk, solidity, which they did not have before. They were far more visible now and there were far more of them. Even the ones which were a good way off were brighter. It was obvious, as well, that they had been planted in rows. If you positioned yourself next to one and looked past it you could see a dozen more, glowing, almost like a fence that could keep nothing out, that let everything through, namely the sunlight and the wind. In each direction there were poles arranged in some kind of grid. The sun was sinking fast and everything began changing fast. The silver poles glowed goldly. It was possible to see the extent of the grid, to see where it ended. There was a clear demarcation now between the area where there were poles and the area where there were no poles, even though the poles were arranged so sparsely and sparingly as to have made the distinction imperceptible at first.

Steve said, 'It's the perfect temperature, except it's about twenty degrees too cold.' But at least the wind was no longer a factor. The wind had left. Now there were just the still poles. It seemed that a very short time after Steve had said what he said we were all spread out again. Everything was still. Everyone could see everyone else. The nearest person to me was Anne, who had spent the last hour walking round with a champagne glass in her hand like a guest at the most poorly attended party ever. Her glass, for most of that hour, had been empty.

The sky grew bluer, was becoming dark, and the poles now were absolutely solid. There was a sense—all the more palpable in such a remote and empty place—of something *gathering*. We were in the midst of what may once have been considered a variety of religious experience. Absence had given way to presence.

The sky blackened and we retreated indoors. We ate quesadillas and drank dark wine and looked at the flames of the pellet-burning stove as if it were a television. The vastness outside made the interior of the cabin seem the coziest place on earth, like an igloo but made of wood and not even chilly.

Later we went outside again, into the huge night. The poles were gone, but we knew they were there. The sky was nothing but a dome of stars. We'd all been in star-

studded places before, were no strangers to the firma-
ment, but none of us had seen anything like this. Viewed
from most places on earth, stars tend to be overhead.
Here they poured down all around to our ankles, even
though they were millions of light-years away. I am not
entirely clear about astronomy, but it seemed possible
that the Milky Way was obscured by the abundance of
stars. The constellations were complicated by passenger jets, blinking planes, flashing satellites: rush hour in
the era of interplanetary travel. The sky was frantic, the
night as cold as old starlight.

I woke as the uncurtained window turned grey. Three
of us met outside. It was colder than ever, as cold as the
Antarctic on the nicest day of the year. The sun was
peeping over the mountaintops. As at sundown, the tips
of the poles began to blink and twinkle. Then, as the
sun emerged into view, the poles stood stark and golden,
even more sharply defined than they had been the evening before. We could see everything now, in all its clarity. This was not just because of the light. It was also,
Cristina said, because we now knew what we were looking for.

When we emerged again, after breakfast, the poles
were less prominent, on the way to becoming almost
invisible, as they had been when we arrived. That was
our first revelation: that while the grid was completely
static it unfolded over time as well as in space. A narrative was at work.

. . .

People like us came and observed versions of this sequence every day for six months of every year. A day was the measure of what went on here. The experience was affected by the weather, the seasons, but not by the larger movement of the planets and stars. Places like Stonehenge had been designed with the solstice in mind, may even have been celestial calendars, attempting to synch man's experience on earth with the heavens. None of that was relevant here. The placement of poles referred to nothing other than itself. Thousands of years of study would confirm that there was no intended relation between the poles and the position of the sun, the transit of Venus or lunar eclipses. What was here was entirely man-made and appealed only to man. Unlike some *Chariot of the Gods*–type places—the Nazca Lines in Peru, say—it was designed not to be seen from the air but to be experienced by people, on the ground.

We worked out that there were four hundred poles. Not 399 or 401 or 402. Exactly four hundred. The number, clearly, was no accident. The poles were in straight lines, but the area they covered was not a square. Two sides had sixteen poles and the other two had twenty-five, each 250 feet apart. The area covered was a mile by a kilometre and six metres.

Our final bit of measuring was to confirm what we referred to thereafter as the Ethan-Cristina paradox.

'The poles are all different lengths,' said Cristina (who is tall).

'Because they're all the same height,' said Ethan (who is short).

He was right. They averaged about twenty feet, but the shortest was only fifteen feet, the tallest twenty-six feet nine inches. The variations in length took account of the uneven surface of the land, so that from tip to tip of every pole was this level plane of invisible flatness. Given the precision of all the distances involved, we wondered if this place was a tribute to the god of *measuring*? Did even the richly stocked pantheon of Hinduism include such a deity?

So the question remained. Apart from suggesting that precise measuring could correct the wonkiness of the world, what was this place meant to do? What was its purpose? Where were we?

The last question is easily answered: we were—as you may have guessed by now—near Quemado, at *The Lightning Field,* created by Walter De Maria and completed in 1977. The answer prompts another question—why the subterfuge of inconceivable ignorance?—which, in turn, takes the form of further questions.

A copy of De Maria's obsessively minute inventory and visionary manifesto, 'The Lightning Field: Some Facts, Notes, Data, Information, Statistics, and Statements,' is left in the hut, but even before arriving—and even if their knowledge of the stats is a little hazy—most visitors who come to *The Lightning Field* know roughly what they are in for. But what if we came here and had to try to work it out for ourselves, with no art-historical back-up? Asked about the consequences of the French Revolution, Chou En-lai replied, 'It's too soon to tell.' That's the response that comes to mind when pondering the significance of the great Land Art projects of the late 1960s and 1970s. With their megalomaniacal schemes and gargantuan undertakings—some, like James Turrell's *Roden Crater* in Arizona, or Michael Heizer's *City* in Nevada, still uncompleted after more than forty years—these artists were thinking big, not just in size and space but in *time*. If they succeed, the best of their undertakings have more in common with sacred or prehistoric sites than with the rival claims and fads of contemporary art. The art stuff provides an immediate context, but it is more revealing to take a different and larger perspective.

One of the most obvious things is as easily overlooked as the poles in the middle of the afternoon: everything about *The Lightning Field* suggests that it will be here for many years to come. So what if we visited the site years hence and had to try to figure out for ourselves what was happening here, what forces were at work, with no art-historical context (minimalism, conceptualism, taking work out of the gallery into the expanded field, etc.)? Enlarging the time scale still further, what if *The Lightning Field* survived after there were people left to see it? How long would it take an alien intelligence—or, to put it another way, how intelligent would an alien have to be—to work out what was going on here? (Could that be the simple mark of genius: when something is easier to conceive and create than it is to work out *how* it was done?)

One thing present-day visitors tend not to know about *The Lightning Field*—or are reluctant to accept—is that it is naïve, even a little vulgar, to expect *lightning*. We came in early May, on only the second day that *The Lightning Field* had been open for the season, but even during the peak period of storm activity, July to September, lightning strikes are exceptional. De Maria spent years searching for an appropriate spot, somewhere with a high incidence of storms. He estimated that there are 'approximately sixty days per year when thunder and lightning activity can be witnessed from The Lightning Field.' I don't know if any record has been kept of the number of lightning storms that have converged on the field itself, but you would count yourself very lucky if you happened to witness what must, surely, be one of the greatest shows on earth. De Maria has rightly insisted that the light is every bit as important as the light*ning* ('the invisible is real'), but calling it *The Lightning Field* was a sensational bit of marketing. Does any artwork have a more electrifying name?

The fact that lightning so rarely appears does not detract from the intended purpose and effect of a place that is helpfully understood in Heideggerian terms. Seeking to explain the relationship of man-made objects to the surrounding landscape in 'Building Dwelling Thinking' Heidegger writes that a bridge 'does not just connect banks that are already there. The banks emerge as banks only as the bridge crosses the stream. The bridge expressly causes them to lie across from each other.' From this it follows that the bridge effectively brings or leads the stream to flow under it and between these banks. 'The bridge *gathers* the earth as landscape around the stream. Thus it guides and attends the stream through the meadows.'

The tail wags the dog in similar and, for our purposes, more explicit fashion in 'The Origin of the Work of Art,' where Heidegger insists that a temple standing on rocky ground draws up out of the rock its 'bulky yet spontaneous support.' Furthermore, the building does not just hold its ground against the storm raging around it but 'first makes the storm itself manifest in its violence.' And not only that: 'The lustre and gleam of the stone, though itself apparently glowing only by the grace of the sun, first brings to radiance the light of the day, the breadth of the sky, the darkness of the night. The temple's firm towering *makes visible the invisible space of air.*' [My italics.]

Notwithstanding this extraordinary sense of cause-generating effect, over the years voices have occasionally dissented from the consensually reverent view of De Maria's achievement. The Dia Art Foundation (which administers the site) controls access to *The Lightning Field* and which photographs of it can appear in print. You can't just drop in, take a quick look and drive off. You have to stay the night, and since the cabin accommodates only six people, you have to book well in advance. Taking aim at these 'authoritarian' measures in a briefly notorious essay, a critic named John Beardsley claimed that the build-up helped 'insure that one will fully expect to see God at the *Lightning Field*. Needless to say, He doesn't appear. No artwork could live up to this hype.'

Except it could and it does. Even without the bonus of lightning, the experience of *The Lightning Field* transcends its reputation. Of course god does not appear. There's a lot of space but, even as a figure of speech, there's no room for god. *The Lightning Field* offers an intensity of experience that for a long time could be articulated only—or most conveniently—within the language of religion. Faced with huge experiences, we have a tendency to fall to our knees, because it's a well-rehearsed expression of awe. Nothing about *The Lightning Field* prompts one to genuflect in this way. Considering some archaeological sites, Lewis Mumford concluded, quite reasonably, 'It is only for their gods that men exert themselves so extravagantly.' *The Lightning Field* represents an absolute refutation or, more precisely, the expiration of that claim—unless art has now become a god. Rigorously atheistic, geometrically neutral, it takes the faith and vaulting promise of modernism into the wilderness. Part of the experience of coming here is the attempt to understand and articulate one's responses *to* the experience.

Also, contrary to Beardsley's griping, access is arranged in such a way as to maximise this experience. You leave your cars at Quemado and are taken up, in a group, at two-thirty in the afternoon. The drive takes half an hour, so you arrive at the least impressive time of the day. As we approached, a groan of disappointment swept through our party: we didn't know exactly what we were expecting but we expected *more*. More what? More *something*. And then, gradually, you get it. You realize that this is not a piece of art to be *seen* but—the point bears repeating—an experience of space that unfolds over time.

This is one of the reasons why *The Lightning Field* is almost unphotographable. It is too spread out—and it takes too long. Everyone sees the same picture—the one on the cover of Robert Hughes's *American Visions*—of a lightning storm dancing round the poles. That is what might be called the *Lightning Field* moment. Lightning may be rare in actuality, but it is right that *The Lightning Field* should be represented in this way. Every other attempt to reduce it to an image, a moment, sells it short.

Within the agreed limits of your visit—you're taken up there and brought back—you can do whatever you like. Few religious sites permit such freedom of behaviour and response. You can drop acid. You can run around naked. You can drink a ton of beer and watch your woman pole-dance. You can sit on the porch reading about the *Spiral Jetty*. You can chant. You can chat with your friends. You can listen to music on your iPod, or you can just stand there with your hands in your pockets, shivering, wishing you'd brought gloves and a scarf. And then you have to leave.

We were picked up at eleven o'clock and driven back to Quemado. In a couple of hours the next bunch of pilgrims would be taken up there. If it hadn't been for them—if it hadn't been booked—we would all have stayed another night, for a week, for the whole summer.

As it was, we ate cherry pie in the El Sarape café and took some pictures to prove we'd all been here together. There's a dusty Ping-Pong table in the otherwise deserted Dia office. Ethan and I played a couple of games before we all headed out of town.

4

Thinking about places like the Hump, the Devil's Chimney,
The Lightning Field *(or, for that matter, sites such as Ang-*
kor Wat or Borobudur), I keep coming back to the painting
that I saw in the Museum of Fine Arts in Boston on the day
I'd hoped to see Gauguin's Where Do We Come From?
What Are We? Where Are We Going? *Elihu Vedder's* The
Questioner of the Sphinx *(1863) shows a dark-skinned*
wanderer or traveller, ear pressed against the head of the
sphinx that emerges from the sea of sand in which it has
been submerged for centuries. Apart from a few broken col-
umns and a human skull (an earlier questioner?), nothing
besides remains. In a way it's an early depiction of the post-
apocalyptic world (the sky is black but it doesn't seem like
night), a reminder, painted in the midst of the American
Civil War, that plenty of civilizations before our own have
suffered apocalyptic extinction. One could easily imagine
that it's not the head of the sphinx poking above the sand
but the torch of the Statue of Liberty, Planet of the Apes–
style. Vedder was in his twenties when he did this paint-
ing. He had not been to Egypt but had seen illustrations of

the Sphinx at Gizeh. His painting seems emblematic of the experiences that crop up repeatedly in this book: of trying to work out what a certain place—a certain way of marking the landscape—means; what it's trying to tell us; what we go to it for.

Time in Space

Maybe it is not the natives of Texas or Arizona who fully appreciate the scale of the places where they have grown up. Perhaps you have to be British, to come from 'an island no bigger than a back garden'—in Lawrence's contemptuous phrase—to grasp properly the immensity of the American West. So it's not surprising that Lawrence considered New Mexico 'the greatest experience from the outside world that I have ever had.'

The cramped paradox of English life: a tiny island that is often hard and sometimes impossible to get around. You can imagine a prospective visitor from Arizona studying a map of England and deciding, 'Yep, we should be able to do this little puppy in a couple of days.' But how long does it take to travel from Gloucester to Heathrow? Anything from two and a half hours to . . . Well, best to allow five to be on the safe side.

In the American West you can travel hundreds of miles and calculate your arrival time almost to the minute. We had turned up for our rendezvous in Quemado at one o'clock on the dot. From Quemado, Jessica and I drove 450 miles to Springdale, on the edge of Zion, in Utah. There were just two of us now, a husband-and-wife team, and we got to Springdale exactly on time for our dinner reservation. After a couple of nights in Zion we headed to the *Spiral Jetty*.

Yes, the *Spiral Jetty*—the wholly elusive grail of Land Art! Instantly iconic, it was transformed into legend by a double negative: the disappearance of the *Jetty* a mere two years after it was created, followed, a year later, by the premature death of its creator, Robert Smithson. Water levels at the Great Salt Lake in northern Utah were unusually low when the Jetty was built in 1970. When the water returned to its normal depth the *Jetty* went under. On 20 July 1973, Smithson was in a light aircraft, reconnoitering a work in progress in Amarillo, Texas. The plane ploughed into a hillside, killing everyone onboard: the pilot, a photographer, and the artist. Smithson was thirty-five. After the *Jetty* sank and his plane crashed, Smithson's reputation soared.

For a quarter of a century the *Spiral Jetty* was all but invisible. There were amazing photographs of the coils of rock in the variously coloured water—reddish, pink, pale blue—and there was the Zapruder-inflected footage of its construction, but the *Jetty* had gone the way of Atlantis, sinking beneath the waveless waves of the Salt Lake. Then, in 1999, a miracle occurred. Excalibur-like, it emerged from the lake. And not only that. The *Jetty* was made out of earth and black lumps of basalt (six and a half thousand tonnes of it), but during the long interval of its submersion it had become covered in salt crystals. In newly resurrected form, it was pristine glittering white.

Even now, after this spectacular renaissance, the *Spiral Jetty* is not always visible. If there is exceptionally heavy snowfall, then the thaw does for the lake what the globally heated polar ice pack threatens to do to the oceans. Once the snowmelt ends up in the lake, it can take months of drought and scorch to boil off the excess and leave the *Jetty* high and dry again. Was it worth travelling all this way to see something we might not be able to see? Well, pilgrims continued to turn up even during the long years when there was *definitely nothing to see,* so it seemed feeble not to give it a chance. (There is probably a sect of art-world extremists who maintain that the best time to have visited the *Spiral Jetty* was during the years of its invisible submergence, when the experience became a pure manifestation of faith.)

We drove north towards Salt Lake City. No need for a compass. Everything screamed north: the grey-and-white mountains looming Canadianly in the distance, the weather deteriorating by the hour. Opting for directness instead of scenery, we barrelled up the featureless expanse of I-15. Most of what there was to see was traffic-related: gas-station logos, trucks the size of freight trains, snakeskin shreds of tire on the soft ('hard' in England) shoulder. Salt Lake City did its bit, its level best, coming to meet us well before we got anywhere near it—and not quite saying goodbye even when we thought we'd got beyond it.

With all the space out west there's no incentive for

cities *not* to sprawl. In the case of Salt Lake City, mountains to the east and the lake to the west mean it does most of its sprawl along a north-south ribbon. Still, there was room for the interstate to gradually assume the width, frenzy—and, eventually, stagnation—of a Los Angeles freeway. Salt Lake City merged, imperceptibly, into Ogden, where we were staying. Not a bad place: fringed by Schloss Adler mountains in at least two directions and looking, on 25th Street at least, as if it was making a *Spiral Jetty*-style comeback from a downturn in fortunes still afflicting other parts of town. Or maybe it was just the alpine winter, which, even in mid-May, had still not shot its wad. Trees weren't convinced they'd got the all-clear; leaf-wise, none of them were venturing out.

In the hotel I read again Lawrence's essay about Taos. Whereas 'some places seem temporary on the face of the earth,' Lawrence believed, 'some places seem final':

Taos pueblo still retains its old nodality. Not like a great city. But, in its way, like one of the monasteries of Europe. You cannot come upon the ruins of the old great monasteries of England, beside their waters, in some lovely valley, now remote, without feeling that here is one of the choice spots of the earth, where the spirit dwelt. To me it is so important to remember that when Rome collapsed, when the great Roman Empire fell into smoking ruins, and bears roamed in the streets of Lyon and wolves howled in the deserted streets of Rome, and Europe really was a dark ruin, then, it was not in castles or manors or cottages that life remained vivid. Then those whose souls were still alive withdrew together and gradually built monasteries, and these monasteries and convents, little communities of quiet labour and courage, isolated, helpless, and yet never overcome in a world flooded with devastation, these alone kept the human spirit from disintegration, from going quite dark, in the Dark Ages. These men made the Church, which again made Europe, inspiring the martial faith of the Middle Ages.

Taos pueblo affects me rather like one of the old monasteries. When you get there you feel something final. There is an arrival.

What a piece of writing and thinking! It's as off-the-cuff as Kerouac; it's analytical, hypnotic, profound, and you get the impression that Lawrence wrote the whole thing—in 1923—without giving it so much as a second thought. Like Vedder's painting, it tells us so much about the power that some places exert and why we go to them. In their different ways, both De Maria and Smithson were attempting to *create* nodality.

The weather in the morning, as we prepared for our assault on the *Jetty*, was not auspicious: sagging cloud, hardly any light and, the moment we drove off, drizzle. On the way out of town we got stuck behind a *Dirty Harry* school bus. By the time we were back on I-15 it was pouring.

We turned off the interstate at Brigham City, heading

towards Corinne, a small farming community. It already felt far more remote, in atmosphere, than it was distant in miles—like Snowdonia or Mull, and just as soggy and drear. The sky was heavy with grey but at least it was only leaking now, not properly raining. Khaki-coloured hills crawled out from beneath a tarpaulin of cloud. The route to the *Jetty* took us through the Golden Spike National Historic Site, commemorating the spot where the two parts of the first transcontinental railroad met in 1869. It was at this point that we began participating in our own form of interactive art commentary.

Smithson was the prime mover in the Land Art scene: not just creating work but organizing exhibitions, setting out credos, proselytising, writing reviews and providing dense theoretical cover for the whole Earth Works hustle. He was a prolific, even torrential writer, and an omnivorous reader. For current tastes he was a tad too caught up in what might be called the discursive practice of the day, but his writing is replete with moments of compelling lucidity and sustained flights of pragmatically visionary appeal. The cover photograph of his *Collected Writings* shows the artist on the *Jetty*, gazing dialectically at his own reflection, looking like Jim Morrison, or like Val Kilmer when he played Morrison in the Oliver Stone movie, embodying his motivating ideas of taking art out of the museum and into the open. Keeping faith with this strategy, I had read out and recorded Smithson's account of his own first trip here and burned it onto a CD to play on the car stereo. As we drove, we listened to this weirdly Anglicised Smithson describing the landscape through which we were passing.

'The valley spread into an uncanny immensity unlike the other landscapes we had seen. . . . Sandy slopes turned into viscous masses of perception. Slowly, we drew near to the lake, which resembled an impassive faint violet sheet held captive in a stony matrix, upon which the sun poured down its crushing light. . . . A series of seeps of heavy black oil more like asphalt occur just south of Rozel Point. For forty or more years people have tried to get oil out of this natural tar pool. Pumps coated with black stickiness rusted in the corrosive salt air. . . . This site gave evidence of a succession of man-made systems mired in abandoned hopes.'

The irony is that in February 2008, Dia organized a petition opposing plans by Pearl Montana Exploration and Production to drill boreholes in the Great Salt Lake—the latest, in other words, in a long history of attempts 'to get oil' that was part of Smithson's original fascination with the area. Which means that the campaign to protect the *Spiral Jetty* is, in some ways, at odds with the convergence of inspiration and circumstance that led to its construction.

We had been given enigmatically precise directions on how to find the *Spiral Jetty*—'Another .5 miles should bring you to a fence but no cattle guard and no gate'—only to find that the route was discreetly signposted. The gravel road was corrugated, washboarded. We jolted and rattled at fifteen miles an hour, past calves the size of big dogs, and cows the size of cows, all of them black and resigned to their lot. The sky slumped over a landscape at once monotonous and always subtly changing. There were constant reminders of Britain, the Dartmoor feeling of worn-down ancientness. Seagulls too. Wordsworth might have had this place in mind when he wrote of 'visionary dreariness.' Suddenly there was a brown cow—the black sheep of the family—and, to the south, in a gap between low, dull hills, a pale glow. Light bouncing off the salt flats? That, in any case, was where we were headed.

We drove more and more slowly as the potholes and trenches increased in width, depth and frequency. The road continued to deteriorate until it gave up any claim to being a road. We left the cocoon of the car, began walking. There had been no signs for a while but there were, allegedly, three things to look out for as markers: an abandoned trailer, an old Dodge truck and—interestingly—an amphibious landing craft. No sign of any of them. But that glow we'd noticed earlier? It wasn't just the reflection on the lake; the sky itself was brightening. To our left the lake looked congealed, like a dead ocean on a used-up planet. There was a faint smell of sulphur. It was a location that might have been scouted for the closing scenes of Cormac McCarthy's *The Road,* where the shining sea turns out to be a further extent of desolation. Protruding from the lake's edge were the remains of some kind of enterprise, long since aborted. Was *that* the *Spiral Jetty*? If it was, then it was in far worse shape than we'd anticipated, not exactly a spiral and barely a jetty at all. There had recently been a certain amount of debate as to whether to try to preserve the *Jetty*, to raise it up and stop it disappearing again or just leave it to its own devices, to decay gracefully and commend itself to the shallow-looking deep. But no, it couldn't be *that* far gone. *Could* it? We kept walking in a state of foiled uncertainty: had we already *had* the experience we were eagerly anticipating?

No. Because there it was, a ring of black rocks—not white, and far smaller than expected but exuding unmistakable *Spiral Jetty*-ness. Smithson warned that size is not the same as scale, that 'size determines an object, but scale determines art.' Fair enough, but I'd seen photographs with people—those centuries-old indicators of scale—on the *Jetty*, dwarfed by it. In the midst of all this sky and land the real thing was quite homely in size and scale. Unlike *The Lightning Field*, the *Spiral Jetty* looked better in photographs than it did in the rocky flesh.

We walked towards the circles of stone, could see that these circles were actually part of an unbroken spiral. This was the *Spiral Jetty*. We were no longer *coming* to the *Spiral Jetty*. We were *at* the *Spiral Jetty*, waiting for the uplift, the feeling of arrival—not just in the getting-there sense but in the way Lawrence had experienced it at Taos Pueblo. And it sort of happened. The weather had been quietly improving. The sky, in places, had turned from lead to zinc. Patches of blue appeared. And now, for the first time that day, the sun came out. There were shadows, light, a slow release of colour.

We clambered down to the *Jetty*—there was no path—through a slope of black rocks where someone had fly-tipped an exhausted mattress. The *Jetty* extended in a long straight spur before bending inwards. The water was plaster-coloured, slightly pink, changing colour as it was enfolded by the spiral, at its whitest in the middle of the coil.

We had hoped the *Jetty* would be visible. Not only was it visible—you could walk on it too. The magical coating of white crystal was largely gone, rubbed off, presumably, by people like us tramping all over it. But what's the alternative? You can't cordon it off like some relic in a museum, so we did our bit in helping to take off the residual shine, further restoring the *Jetty* to its original condition. Compared with Angkor Wat and the pyramids, the *Jetty* was not doing too well. It had aged at the rate of the rain-smeared concrete of the Southbank Centre or council estates done on the cheap and put up in a hurry. In less than forty years it already looked ancient. Which, actually, is the best thing about it. *The Lightning Field* looks perpetually sci-fi; in next to no time, the *Spiral Jetty* had acquired the bleak gravity and elemental aura of prehistory. It would be easy to believe that it had been built millennia ago by the people who first settled here—but why would they have settled *here* of all places?

The artist John Coplans wrote that entering the spiral involved walking counter-clockwise, going back in time; exiting, you go forward again. That's true, part of the conceptual underpinning of the experience. But he forgot another, no less important, lesson of perambulatory physics, what might be called the Law of Sink Estate Directness. At Downing College, Cambridge, signs—and hundreds of years of observed convention—warn that only Fellows may walk on the grass. Rather than walk across the prairie-size quad, you have to take a frustrating detour around the edges. In less august settings any attempt at decoration or elaboration that involves lengthening people's journey time is destined to fail. Rather than walk two sides of a square—even if it is named after Byron or Max Roach—people will cut across it diagonally, lugging orange-bagged souvenirs of their pilgrimage to Sainsbury's cathedral, creating their own, urban version of a Richard Long. Before long—or *contra* Long—the grass starts to wear out and a so-called 'desire path' is formed. Same here. Although the stretches between the spiraling rock were underwater, the salt beds were soggy but firm. So you didn't need to walk around the spiral, you could just step across! Why walk back in time when you can jump-cut across it in a flash? In moments you are at the end of the spiral—the dead centre of the space-time continuum, the still point of the turning world.

Near this centre earlier visitors had arranged rocks and stones so that they spelled out names in the white salt of the enclosed lake bed: missy (with a heart underneath), ida marie and estelle.

The sky continued to open up. With the sound of birds and lapping water, it was lovely in a subdued and desolate way. It felt abandoned but it was not a place of abandoned meaning. It had retained—or generated— its own dismal nodality. The answer to the obvious question—was it worth coming all this way?—might have been no, but it didn't occur to us to ask. The *Spiral Jetty* was here. We were here. That was the simple truth. Could the more complex truth be that if it wasn't so difficult to get to no one would bother coming to see it?

André Malraux famously cherished the idea of a

museum without walls. In a way, places like the *Spiral Jetty* are *jails* without walls. They are always about time, about how long they can detain or hold you. I remember the governor of a U.S. prison saying, of a particularly violent inmate, that he already had way more time than he'd ever be able to do. That's exactly how the *Jetty* looked—like it already had more time than it could ever do—even though, relatively speaking, it had hardly begun to put in any serious time.

In uncertain tribute, we stayed longer than we needed to, waiting for any potential increments of the experience to make themselves felt. One or the other of us kept saying, 'Shall we go?' and, in this way, our visit was gradually extended. Nothing happened except the slow erosion of urgency and purpose. We were often ready to leave, but every time we thought about leaving we remembered the previous time we had thought about leaving and were glad the urge had not been acted on.

And then, eventually, without a word, when the desire to leave was all but extinguished, we began walking back to the car. The air was irritable with sandflies. I almost trod on a long, grey, indifferent snake. The lone and level lake stretched far away.

5

Sites such as those painted by Vedder are not always mired in the sands of the past: they are still coming into existence, are continually being created, even if they cannot always be seen—as when a construction worker mixed a Boston Red Sox T-shirt into concrete that was being poured into part of the new Yankee Stadium in the Bronx, aiming to curse it.

In a photograph taken by Chaiwat Subprasom in 2014, we can see the very beginning of the processes at work in the formation of one such potential site. At first glance it seems a nice if rather pointless holiday snap. More accurately, a photograph of people taking a rather pointless holiday snap. In this respect it—the snap—is exemplary, since 90 percent of the pictures now being taken are pointless. The weather is fine, the beach is nice, the water is a gentle, unthreatening turquoise, but it's not as if the rock in the middle is covered in ancient petroglyphs or even graffiti. That leaves the dog. A nice enough doggy, to be sure, and there's always something fun about a dog at the seaside—until it comes trotting back and leaves sand and saltwater all over your sofa . . .

Except this is the beach on Koh Tao in Thailand where the bodies of two murdered British tourists had been discovered two weeks earlier. This knowledge changes everything—including our perception of the dog, who now seems to have sensed or scented something untoward. In its modest way the picture being taken by the woman in the bikini recalls Joel Sternfeld's photographs of parking lots or street corners in On This Site: *unremarkable spots transformed into photographic memorials by captions explaining that these are places where a rape, murder or abduction took place. The couple in the photograph probably offered a similar explanatory caption when they showed the picture to friends or posted it on Tumblr. Still, their picture was not anything like as interesting as this one: a photograph showing the transformation being made. It is the act—her act—of taking the picture that invests the site with meaning. Her picture might be pointless; the act of taking it is not. Quite possibly she is taking it not to make a visual record but to offer some kind of tribute, to pay her respects in the way that, had any been available, she might have left a bunch of flowers. This is often the case: people don't take pictures in order to have a picture; they take pictures because that is what you do. Perhaps it's better put interrogatively: what else can you do? The man provides the answer: you just stand there.*

People will continue to come to this beach. More photographs will be taken. A memorial to the dead couple will possibly be built or their names carved on the rock. Even if neither happens, some visitors to this spot will be conscious that something has happened here, will be familiar with the story of the murder. And even if that knowledge fades, this spot will still exude a faint charge of uncomprehended—possibly unnoticed—meaning. How long will that charge hold? What will remain of it two hundred years hence?

Northern Dark

Shortly after getting back from Utah, Jessica became obsessed with seeing the Northern Lights. She had been mentioning the Northern Lights for several years but now she began mentioning them all the time, telling me about friends for whom seeing the Northern Lights had been 'the experience of a lifetime.' Other topics were just preludes to the topic of the Northern Lights and how badly she wanted to see them. At one point she claimed that we were probably the only people in the world who had not seen the Northern Lights, that she didn't know why I wouldn't take her to see the Northern Lights. I wanted to see them too, I said. I just didn't see when we would have a chance to go.

'We could go in August,' she said.

'That has got to be among the most stupid things ever said by anyone,' I said. I say stupid things too. We actually spur each other on to see who can come out with the most stupid things, so this was sort of a compliment. 'You have to go in the winter,' I said. 'When it's dark. In the summer it's the land of the midnight sun. It's the old

Kierkegaardian either/or. Either the Northern Lights or the midnight sun. You can't have both.'

'Oh, I see. We can't have both, so we've got to have neither. That's what I call stupid.'

'That's what I call the remark of someone who has no understanding of logic whatsoever,' I said.

This was in May. We weren't really interested in experiencing the midnight sun, though we did enjoy hearing about it from our friend Sjon, who lives in Reykjavik.

'When I was a kid I had trouble sleeping in the summer,' he told us over dinner at an Indian restaurant in London. 'In my twenties, I stayed up partying all night. Now I have very thick curtains.'

The months slipped by, the days grew longer and then, as soon as they had become as long as possible, they started to get shorter, until a day lasted only half a day, and this year became last year and next year became this year and we were suddenly in the fifth year of what Jessica had told Sjon was 'a basically sunless marriage.' Weather-wise, it had been the most severe December in London for over a hundred years. Snow came early, bringing 'travel chaos' to the road and rail networks. Heathrow could not cope. Flights were cancelled, but we were cozy at home, eating biscuits and watching the snow drift past our uncurtained windows or watching the news on TV, glad that we weren't camped out like refugees at Heathrow, waiting out the backlog of cancelled flights, pestering airline staff for the food and drink vouchers to which we were surely entitled. Then, in January, after the snow had cleared and the country was back on its feet again, we *were* there, at Heathrow, waiting for a plane that would take us north, north to Oslo, then further north to Tromsø and deep into the Arctic Circle, to the Svalbard archipelago.

Having opted for the Northern Lights Experience rather than the Midnight Sun Experience, our chances of being able to have the Northern Lights Experience were enhanced by the fact that it was dark all day long. We could spend twenty-four hours a day seeing the Northern Lights, having the Northern Lights Experience, but first we experienced the Expense Experience in Oslo. How lovely it must be to live there and travel elsewhere, to arrive in London, Tokyo or even Papeete and be amazed by how cheap everything is. The train from the airport to the centre of town cost a fortune. Then we walked from our expensive hotel through the frozen city, past the frozen pond or rink where everyone was expertly skating, and ate at the most expensive restaurant in the world even though, by Oslo standards, it was modestly priced. We were stunned by the cold and the expense but not so stunned that we did not feel the first inkling of regret for coming to a frozen, dark and fiendishly expensive country.

In the morning, at paralysing expense, we travelled back to the airport to fly on to Tromsø and Svalbard. A snowstorm was in progress, a storm that would have paralysed England for six months and might even have led to a declaration of a state of emergency and the imposition of martial law. In Oslo the Norwegians took it in their stride. Part of the reason our dinner had been so expensive, I guessed as we sat on the plane, watching its wings get de-iced, must have been taxes which went towards the cost of keeping the travel network unparalysed throughout the blizzards and subzero temperatures that were such a regular feature of life that our take-off was delayed by only five minutes.

It was daylight when we took off and night when we arrived, several hours later, in Longyearbyen. Even if we had landed when we had taken off it would still have been night in Longyearbyen. We could have landed here any time in the previous six weeks and it would have been deep night and it would have been just as cold, colder than anywhere I had ever been, colder and darker than anywhere anyone in their right mind would ever have visited. We had only just got off the plane, were walking to the terminal, when Jessica said exactly what I was thinking:

'Why have we come to this hellhole?'

'Because you wanted to see the Northern Lights,' I said, though at that point there was nothing to see but the Northern Dark, darkness everywhere, all around, with no possibility of light.

A cheerless bus took us from the terminal into the godforsaken town. There was nothing to see, except lights shining in the darkness, revealing—though this seemed hard to credit—people working outside, building buildings in conditions when everything required for building must have been rendered unbuildably useless by the unbelievable cold.

The Basecamp Trapper's Hotel was a deliberately

rough-hewn place, comfortable but sufficiently make-shift to impart a Shackletonian quality to one's stay in the frozen wastes. In the breakfast room there was a polar-bear skin on the wall, like a Raj tiger in vertical mode. Best of all, there was a glass-ceilinged area where you could kick back and trip out on the Northern Lights. An extremely attractive little nook, this, because although we had only been in Longyearbyen about ten minutes that was long enough to disabuse us of the idea that we had come from a country that had endured a harsh winter. We had actually come from a mild, temperate little island, quaintly inexpensive and Mediterranean in its wintery balminess. Nevertheless, we did what you do when you come to a place for a Euro city break: we went for a walk, one of the most horrible walks we had ever embarked on. The Norwegian word for 'stroll' is best translated as 'grim battle for survival': *Ice Station Zebra* stuff, with elements of the retreat from Moscow thrown in. The temperature was a thousand degrees below zero, not counting the wind-chill, which sent snow streaming through the dark streets as if fleeing an invading army. We made it to the harshly lit supermarket, where we bought beer, returned to our room and sat on the bed without speaking. I sensed that the chances of having sex in the course of our stay were, like the temperature, far below zero. We had been here little more than an hour and our spirits were already appreciably lower than they had been in Oslo, to say nothing of London, which we now looked back on with bliss-was-it-in-that-dawn nostalgia.

The Northern Lights were not in evidence that night, the night of our arrival. I say 'that night' but we were in the land of perpetual night, the dark night of the Norwegian soul that would last another month at least. The thing about the Northern Lights, explained one of the cheerful young women who worked at reception and wished to clarify the situation for us before we set out for dinner, is that at this time of year they could appear at any moment, without warning. A state of constant alertness was required even though, it was conceded, on a scale of 1 to 9 the likelihood of their appearing tomorrow was a mere 2. But the day after tomorrow it zoomed up to 3. And it's not like the Northern Lights were the only game in town. We may have come all this way, to 'this frozen fucking hellhole,' as Jessica called it, to see the Northern Lights, but there were other things to do as well. In the morning, for example, the morning that was indistinguishable from night and afternoon, we were going dog mushing.

After our trip to the supermarket we had set out for dinner as though making an assault on the summit of K2. For a morning's dog mushing, however, more serious kit was required: three pairs of socks, thermals, two T-shirts, a lumberjack shirt, a thick sweater—with, rather appropriately, a Norwegian flag on the sleeve—a woollen hat, gloves and an enormous parka. This was my *under*wear. A van picked us up at the hotel and took us, through the awful darkness, to the large expedition HQ, where we hauled on snowsuits, full-face provo balaclavas, ski goggles, snow boots and mittens. Suited and immensely booted, barely able to move, we got back in the van and drove on to the dog yard. There were six of us, Jessica and me, a Romanian couple who had immigrated to Denmark and our two guides, Birgitte and Yeti.

'*Yeti?*' I said. 'What an abominable name!'

The entrance to the dog yard was marked by seal skins hanging on a triangular gallows like a frosty modern artwork in the style of a skeletal wigwam. There were ninety dogs there, ninety Alaskan huskies, chained and yelping in the urine-stained and poo-smeared ice of the compound. Lights, fences and snow all contributed to the impression that we had stumbled into some kind of canine Gulag. Not that the doggies were unhappy or unloved. They were chomping at the bit, straining at the leash. Every dog has its day, and each and every one of these yelpers hoped that this would be his or hers. And that wasn't all that was going on. Implausible though it seemed in such icy conditions, the females, somehow, were *in heat*, and the males were desperate to get their paws on them. To us they were friendly rather than randy, as cuddly as anything, but the yelping was like the soundtrack of a doggy nightmare. They had lovely names, the dogs. Junior, Fifty, Ivory, Mara, Yukon and—though I may have got this wrong—Tampax were among the lucky ones chosen to go out with us on this day that was indistinguishable from deepest night. Although it was dark I could see the huskies' strange eyes, so pale and milky clear that they seemed independent of the bodies in which they were lodged: planets in a dog-shaped universe. Presumably these eyes meant that the dogs had night-vision, could see for miles in the deepest night. I was surrounded by these eyes, cold and flashing with a clarity that seemed devoid of intelligence or even life. Part of our job—part of the day's advertised fun, even though, just as what was called day was really deep night, this fun was pure misery—was to take the selected dogs, put them in harness and fix the harness to the sled, six dogs per sled. The yelping was driving me insane and my toes were already numb with cold. Because I was thinking of my numb toes and constantly checking that not an inch of my flesh was exposed, I was not listening properly to the instructions about how to put the harnesses on, and it was not easy to hear anyway, with my parka and snowsuit hood pulled up and my head full of the sound of the yelping of ninety Alaskan huskies, half of them in heat and all of them desperate to run or fuck or both. The dogs lifted their forelegs to help with the tricky business of clambering into the harness. It was like putting a baby's leg into a romper suit, but a baby with a lifetime's experience of preparing for sledding expeditions in the frozen Arctic. Saddling up the three teams of dogs took ages, partly because with these multiple layers of clothes squashed under one's snowsuit it was possible to move only at the speed of a deep-sea diver. I am tall anyway, but with all this clobber I loomed like death itself in the polar night. Death be not proud! I got into such a tangle with the numerous, often inexplicable bits of harness and rope and the dogs all leaping over each other that I slipped onto my back, landing on the hard ice, which, through all these layers of clothing-blubber, felt as soft as a piss-streaked sponge cake. There is a lesson to be learned from this: in the depths of the darkest night and the darkness of the deepest cold, mankind's need for slapstick will never be quite extinguished.

Eventually, we were saddled up and ready to go. Whenever we hire a car Jessica always steers us out of the parking lot for the first few tentative miles, when we are unsure of the controls and the chances of an accident are at their peak. On this occasion, though, I was driving. I said that she should take the reins, but she insisted that this was my manly prerogative and plonked herself down in the sled on a comfy-looking piece of blue rug. A few moments later we were off. We had not been under starter's orders, but we were off. First team out, second team out—and then us, bringing up the rear in suddenly hot pursuit. The huskies meant business, there was no doubt about that. I still had the sled's anchor in my hand, was struggling to hook it to the side of the sled so that it would not impale Jessica's head like a fishing hook in the cheek of a big human fish. An extraordinary amount of speed had been abruptly unleashed, unharnessed by even a modicum of control. We were charging downhill, at an angle, so we had to lean into the slope to avoid capsizing. Through my hood I could still hear the dogs yelping, though by now my head was so full of yelping this might have been the residue of the old yelping of dogs in the compound, not the ecstatic yelping of huskies galloping through the Arctic dark. It was hard work steering the sled, hard enough to make me sweat. It felt good being hot, but sweating was not good at all, because—I remembered this from Alistair MacLean's appropriately named *Night Without End*—as soon as this exertion was over the sweat would freeze. We were zooming along, plunging down a slope. I lost control of the sled, over which I had never had the slightest control, and tumbled off the back into deep snow. The sled spilled over, but the anchor—which was supposed to serve as a brake—had not been deployed and the huskies did not stop. They had not been released from captivity in order to have their outing curtailed at this early stage. Even through my hood I could hear Jessica yelling 'Stop.' She was dragged for fifty metres, tangled up beneath the sled and, for all I knew, had the anchor embedded in her skull. As I ran after her, with no thought in my head except her welfare, I was silently forming the words 'I *said* you should have driven first.' It took ages to get the attention of the other teams, because they had zoomed off even faster than we had. Eventually, Birgitte and Yeti came back and pulled the sled off Jessica. She was uninjured but sufficiently shaken up to declare that she did not want to go on. I had actually enjoyed getting thrown from the sled in the same way that, years earlier, I'd enjoyed getting thrown out of the raft when I was white-water rafting along the Zambezi in conditions that, meteorologically, were the polar opposite of those here, in the deep night of the Arctic soul. We were all standing with our breath creating little snowstorms in the light of our headlamps, busy disentangling all the reins and dogs, which had got into the most incredible tangle. I say 'we' but I just stood there, doing nothing, sweating and breathing heavily,

Salzburg, 1977 by Luigi Ghirri
(Copyright © Eredi di Luigi Ghirri)

The Questioner of the Sphinx by Elihu Vedder
(Oil on canvas, photograph copyright © Museum of Fine Arts, Boston)

Koh Tao, 2014 by Chaiwat Subprasom
(Reuters/Chaiwat Subprasom)

Muscle Beach, Los Angeles by Frank Thomas
(Photograph courtesy of the Frank J. Thomas Archives)

worrying that, if I exerted myself further, I would end up entombed like the Frankenstein monster in a glacier of frozen sweat. Actually, I did try to do something: I tried to take pictures of what I referred to as 'the crash site,' but my camera had frozen. Everything about this environment was quite unsuited to photography, human habitation, tourism or happiness. Jessica had had enough too, was persuaded to continue only on condition that she was driven by Yeti or Birgitte and not by 'that idiot.'

'She's in shock,' I said. 'She doesn't know what she's saying.' I had no desire to drive either, and so we both ended up as passengers, each on a sled driven by one of the guides. We made much better progress like this.

And it wasn't pitch black, I could see now. There was a glimmer of dark light around the dark contours of the mountains or whatever they were, and a glimmer of stars, but the overwhelming impression was that there was nothing to see. My toes were still numb but, despite my fears about freezing sweat, I was surprisingly warm, especially when I discovered that the blue rug Jessica had been sitting on was actually a kind of mini–sleeping bag and I was able to add yet another layer of insulation. Bundled up like this, like a frozen mummy, it was quite fun, barrelling through the barren wastes. I didn't have much on my mind except for thinking how much better it would have been to do this in the mystic twilight of February, when you could actually see where you were, but at least there was a suggestion of light in the sky, even if, by any normal definition of the phrase, it was still pitch dark. Oh, and I had come to love the huskies.

Irrespective of what the job entails, I love anyone—man or beast—who does their job well, and these huskies, whose job was to pull a sled, were absolute in their huskiness. From reading about Amundsen's expedition to the South Pole I knew that, if the going got tough, the huskies could be fed to each other. Yeti kept up a lovely sing-song of instruction and encouragement, which, for all I knew, constantly reminded the dogs of this fact, that the weak would become food for the less weak. So has it always been, so will it always be! Since she was singing I started singing too, one of the cadence songs from *Full Metal Jacket*: 'I don't know but I been told . . . *I don't know but I been told* . . . Eskimo pussy is mighty cold.' And then I thought of the film *Atanarjuat* (*The Fast Runner*), which, among its many other virtues, hotly refutes this claim. My mind was wandering, but it kept coming back to the immediate reality, which was that we were out in the open air, in pitch darkness—the brief period when a glimmer of dark light appeared on the horizon had already come to an end, was no more than a memory now—in freezing conditions, and that the Northern Lights were nowhere to be seen.

It took an hour to get back to the dog yard, back to the infernal but adorable yapping of the dogs, both those who had been out, who had had their day, and those who had not, who hoped their day was still to come, still to be had. We had to de-harness our dogs and return them to their kennels, but I didn't even make the pretence of helping. I just stood around, thinking about my cold feet, letting the guides do the donkey work for which they were, after all, being paid—and paid hand-

somely if they were able to survive the punishing expense
of living in Norway, even if this meant they were only
paid the minimum wage, which must have been about a
hundred grand a year. Once the dogs were back in their
kennels we tramped over to the cozy trappers' cabin. Just
as the so-called 'light' in the sky had actually been dark,
so, by any normal standards, it was freezing cold in the
cabin, but, relatively speaking, it was toasty. The talk, as
we drank hot coffee, was of frostbite. If you get bitten
in your cheek you place a hand there but you don't rub,
you hold your warm hand to your cheek—assuming, of
course, that your hand is not a solid lump of blood-ice
too. Birgitte and Yeti were both in their early twenties
and they loved it up here in the winter.

'Why?' I asked, and it was obvious that the single
word was followed, inaudibly, by two others: *on earth,*
as in *Why on earth would anyone want to spend their time
in a hellhole like this?* Well, they liked the social life and
the slow return of daylight. And today had been a joyous
experience for them. Birgitte had been away on vacation
for ten days. When she had last been out here there was
no light at all; today there had been a glimmer. So the
polar night, though still immense, was receding. There
was light at the end of the tunnel.

'Which still begs the question,' Jessica said later, 'of
why anyone would choose to live in a *tunnel.*'

We spent the so-called 'afternoon' in our room. Jessica
told me about the Annie Dillard essay she was reading,
about polar explorers and the solemn reserve of the prose

in which their adventures were recounted. Dillard wonders if this was part of the selection process—'or even
if some eminent Victorians, examining their own prose
styles, realized, perhaps dismayed, that from the look
of it, they would have to go in for polar exploration.'
I remember making a cautionary mental note about
that—*Avoid solemn splendour*—after which I don't know
what I did. I think I had frostbite of the brain or something, because I just sat there and thawed—thawed about
nothing—until it was time to head out to the bar of the
nearby Radisson Hotel for dinner. In any normal part of
the world this would have involved a ten-minute walk,
but by now the idea that places existed where the simple
act of *stepping outside* did not require careful preparation and planning seemed quaintly implausible. It was
the coldest and darkest night in the entire history of the
planet, possibly of any planet. I looked up occasionally
in case the Northern Lights showed up, but mainly I
kept my eyes on the ground in case I slipped.

The bar of the Radisson was awash with information and rumour about the Northern Lights. Tourists
and residents all had their stories. The Lights could be
seen at any time, but the best chance was in the evening.
From six o'clock onwards. Others said there was more
chance of activity from about eleven onwards. I liked
this word 'activity' with its suggestion of the paranormal,
but mainly I liked the way that it was being said inside a
restaurant. Then someone claimed that we were actually
too far *north* for the Northern Lights. We were feeling
confused and more than a bit dejected, so it was reas-

suring to hear the barman announce that they would now be showing, on a large-screen TV, live football from the Premiership. Arsenal–Man City! Fuck the Northern Lights with their unscheduled, possibly even mythical appearances. This floodlit game was *scheduled* and was going ahead on time, exactly as advertised. The bar filled up. Midway through the second half, the barmaid, who had nipped outside for a cigarette, told us the Northern Lights were happening. We dashed outside. There was a faint glimmer in the general night-glimmer, but light pollution from the town meant that we could see almost nothing. We went back in and watched the rest of the football, unsure whether to feel relieved—because we were back inside, out of the cold, or depressed because, although we could watch Premiership games any old time, this was our only chance to have the once-in-a-lifetime experience of the Northern Lights Experience.

In the so-called 'morning' the cheerful young woman at Basecamp reception asked if we had seen the Northern Lights the night before.

'No,' I said, 'but we did see the football!' I was only joking even if, strictly speaking, I wasn't joking. I was actually deeply disappointed, but, in a weird Nordic turnaround, we had become the *source* of disappointment to our hosts. The implication was clear: not seeing the Northern Lights was a result not of their non-appearance but a failure on our part, a failure of perception and atti-tude. Finding this a little hard to take, I found myself saying that I 'took umbrage' at such a claim, even though this was a phrase I never normally use. It was like *If you're going to get all Norwegian-mystic with me, young lady, I'll get all middle-England-tourist with you,* even if this amounted to standing there looking downcast and crest-fallen. We wanted to see the Northern Lights. We had come all this way, to this blighted place, to see the North-ern Lights. We came at what, from every other point of view, was a ghastly time of the year, to see the Northern Lights. But seeing the Northern Lights can apparently be a much subtler affair than the photographs—swirling geysers of psychedelic green—lead one to expect. Some-times they are so subtle that your eyes and mind have to be attuned. Seeing is believing—and believing is see-ing. Once you have seen the Northern Lights—once you know what you are looking for—you believe you can see them again. In this respect it reminded me of early attempts to get stoned (which in turn reminded me that there is a famous strain of pure indica called Northern Lights). You could not get stoned—this was in the days before skunk, before you knew without doubt that your brains were in the process of being blown out—until you knew what it was like to be stoned. The more conversa-tions we had, the more the Northern Lights—which, I had assumed, came as standard in this part of the world, at this time of the year—took on some of the unverifi-able allure of the Loch Ness Monster or the Abominable Snowman.

Our spirits worsened. There seemed a correlation between the lack of perceived 'activity' in the skies and our own deepening *in*activity. We skulked in our room, became steadily more cast down and crestfallen. The explanation for this might have been that we had not adapted properly to the extreme cold and the endless night, but the opposite was true. Many visitors apparently enjoy the novelty of three days of Arctic night while finding it hard to believe that anyone could spend years living here. Our responsiveness to Svalbard was so intense that we skipped this honeymoon period and experienced three days as though they were three years—and promptly plunged headlong into the gloom that can gnaw away at people who have spent years here. On the third or fourth morning—which might as well have been the thirtieth or fortieth morning—Yeti knocked on our door so that we'd be ready for the snowmobiling trip that we'd signed up for. I got out of bed, opened the door a crack and told her that we would not be going.

What would have been the point? I said when we saw her again at the reception desk later in the day. The same freezing cold, the same nothing-to-see darkness that we had experienced on the wretched dog-mushing trip. No, thank you very much, I said, before turning on my heel and shuffling back to bed. It was miserable in our room, but it was better than not being in our room.

'The Northern Lights could knock on our door now,' I said to Jessica, 'and I wouldn't even give them the time of day.'

We spent the whole so-called 'day' in our room, downcast and crestfallen, and then, in the so-called 'evening,' forced ourselves up and out into the frozen night. We trudged to the restaurant on the edge of town in the freezing cold and the pitch-dark darkness. There were polar bears in the area, but we had been told that if we kept to the road we would be safe, and at some level polar bears were the least of our worries. As we walked we naturally kept an eye open not only for polar bears but for Northern Lights. We looked. We were ready to believe. We were ready to see. We retained the capacity for belief, but deep down we had started to believe that the Northern Lights, if they existed, would not be seen by us. We chewed our reindeer steaks and trudged back again through the freezing night and the implacable cold. There was nothing to see, and the only point of the walk was for it to be over with, to know that we had not died from it, that we had lived to tell the tale, the tale that eventually became this tale.

We left the following day, empty-handed and empty-eyed. Relations with the people running the Basecamp had become somewhat frosty. My joke about Yeti's name had caught on to the extent that Jessica and I referred to her only as 'the abominable Yeti,' but it had not endeared us to her, and while nothing that had happened since had caused her to feel more warmly towards us quite a few things—not least my singing that song from *Full Metal Jacket*—had contributed to an increased frostiness. We were like skeptics among the faithful at Lourdes and they were glad to see the back of us. That was fine by us, because we were glad to see the back of a place which we had taken to referring to either as 'this ghastly place' or 'this fucking hellhole' before settling on 'abominable' as the adjective of choice. We had had the experience of a lifetime but it was not the experience that we had hoped for; it was like a lifetime of disappointment compressed into less than a week, which actually felt like it had lasted the best—in the sense of worst—part of a lifetime.

The cheerless bus took us back through the abominable city to the airport, to the terminal. Our experience might have been expected to put a strain on our marriage, but the experience of being so thoroughly crestfallen and downcast had made us closer, even though this would not have been obvious to an outsider as we sat silently in the depressing terminal, waiting for the plane, which, to give credit where it is due, took off exactly on time. When we landed at Tromsø an English couple we had met in the bar of the Radisson said, 'Did you see the Northern Lights?' Apparently, the Lights had put in a special guest appearance as we were flying—*but on the other side of the plane.* It was like there was a blight on us, and even though I'd assumed our spirits could not sink any lower they did sink even lower, and then, after we'd changed planes yet again, in Oslo, they sank still lower. I found myself in an unbelievably cramped seat, with zero leg room, in spite of being assured that I had an exit-row seat. The flight attendant—a once-blonde Norwegian woman in her fifties—came by and asked if there was anything we would like. She meant in the way of food and beverages, but after being cooped up in our room in Longyearbyen I started ranting about the seat, the abominable seat with its abysmal lack of leg room, how I was cooped up like a chicken with deep vein thrombosis. Jessica had sunk into a kind of catatonia, did not say anything, but for the first time in several days, like a limb that has been frozen and is coming painfully back to life, I felt energised by my anger and outrage. Unlike the abominable Yeti and the other girls at Basecamp who had taken against us because of our poor attitude, the flight attendant was entirely sympathetic, agreeing that conditions were intolerably cramped for a tall man like me. She gave me some orange juice—free!—and I calmed down, even though, in my head, I continued to formulate expressions of outrage and hard-done-by-ness. And then, as we were about to begin our descent into Heathrow, something extraordinary happened. The flight attendant came back and knelt in the aisle with her hand on my knee. She looked into my crestfallen eyes, the eyes that had not seen the Northern Lights, and said again how uncomfortable I must be, how sorry she was. Without taking her eyes from mine she said that one day I would surely get the seat I deserved, and as she spoke, I believed that this would happen.

6

My mother grew up on a farm in the village of Worthen in Shropshire. I never liked going there to visit my grandparents: house and surrounding countryside shared an atmosphere of dank unhappiness (my grandfather had allegedly been cursed by a Gypsy) but this was not without its own brooding allure. Everything seemed far older than where we lived in Cheltenham. Marton Pool, a nearby lake, was said to be bottomless. It was held to be dangerous, because swimmers could get caught in the reeds that grew on the lake bed. As a boy I was oblivious to what I realize now was not a contradiction but an authentication or verification that this place existed in the realm of the mythic.

I also heard, many times, about the Robber's Grave in the churchyard in Montgomery. As my grandfather and mother told the story, a man had been hanged for stealing a sheep. On the scaffold, insisting on his innocence, he prophesied that if he was telling the truth no grass would grow in an area the shape of a cross on his grave. The execution went ahead, and the sky, which had been clear, grew suddenly dark (a meteorological detail easily dismissed as after-the-

fact atmospheric elaboration). We drove to Montgomery to visit this fabled place when I was about fourteen. The grave was easy to find in the dismal churchyard and, pretty much as claimed, there was a bare patch of ground in a shape approximating a cross—more like a diamond. The grave had become a tourist attraction, and even at that young age I suspected that it was preserved and maintained as such (by weed killer?). Still, the whole package—hearing about this place and visiting it—evidently stayed with me: I wrote about it in my English O-level exam.

White Sands

My wife and I were driving south on Highway 54, from Alamogordo to El Paso. We'd spent the afternoon in White Sands and my brain was still scorched from the glare. I worried that I might even have done some permanent damage to my eyes. The sand is made of gypsum—whatever that is—and is as bright as new-fallen snow. Brighter, actually. It's really quite unbelievable that anything can be so bright. It's a very good name, White Sands, even though we thought the place a bit disappointing at first. The sand was a little discoloured, not quite white. Then, as we drove further, the sand started to creep onto the road and it became whiter, and soon everything was white, even the road, and then there was no road, just this bright whiteness. We parked the car and walked into it, into the whiteness. It was hard to believe that such a place really existed. The sky was pristine blue, but the thing that must be emphasised is the whiteness of the sand, which could not have been any whiter. We would have liked to stay longer in this unstained wilderness, but we had to get to El Paso that night. We walked back to the car and headed out of the park.

Jessica was driving. It was early evening. We were about sixty miles south of Alamogordo and the light was fading. A freight train was running parallel to the road, also heading south.

'Hitchhiker!' I said, pointing. 'Shall we pick him up?'

'Shall we?' Jessica was slowing down. We could see him more clearly now, a black guy, in his late twenties, clean and not looking like a maniac or someone who smelled bad. We slowed to a crawl and took a good look at him. He looked fine. I lowered my window, the passenger window. He had a nice smile.

'Where ya going?' he said.

'El Paso,' I said.

'That'd be great for me.'

'Sure. Get in.'

He opened the door and climbed into the back seat. Our eyes met in the mirror. Jessica said, 'Hi.'

''Preciate it,' he said.

'You're welcome.' Jessica accelerated and soon we were back up to seventy and drawing level once again with the long freight to our left.

'Where've you come from?' I asked, twisting round in my seat. I could see now that he was perhaps older than I had initially thought. He had deep lines in his face, but his eyes were kind and his smile was still nice.

'Albuquerque,' he said. I was slightly surprised. The logical way to have got to El Paso from Albuquerque would have been to go straight down I-25. 'Where you from?' he asked.

'London,' I said. 'England.'

'The Kingdom,' he said.

'Right.' I was facing straight ahead again, because I worried that twisting around in my seat would give me a cricked neck, to which I am prone.

'I thought so,' he said. 'I love your accent.'

'What about you?'

'Arkansas originally.'

'That's where my mother's from,' said Jessica. 'El Dorado, Arkansas. Before she moved to England.'

'I'm from Little Rock,' he said.

'Like Pharoah Sanders,' I said. It was a pointless thing to say, but I have this need to show off, to show that I know things; in this instance to show that I knew about jazz, about black jazz musicians. The guy, evidently, was not a jazz fan. He nodded but said nothing, and we prepared to settle into the occasionally interrupted silence that tends to work best in these situations. We had established where we were from and where we were going, and a pleasant atmosphere filled the car. Then, less than a minute later, this pleasant atmosphere was changed absolutely by a sign:

NOTICE

DO NOT PICK UP HITCHHIKERS

DETENTION FACILITIES IN AREA

I had seen the sign. Jessica had seen the sign. Our hitchhiker had seen the sign. We had all seen the sign, and the sign had changed our relationship totally. What struck me was the plural: not *a* detention facility but detention facilit*ies*. Several of them. The notice—and I took some heart from the fact that the sign described itself as a Notice rather than a Warning—did not specify *how* many, but there were, clearly, more than one. I did not glance at Jessica. She did not glance at me. There was no need, because at some level everyone was glancing at everyone else. As well as not glancing, no one said a word. I have always believed in the notion of the vibe: good vibes, bad vibes. After we saw the sign the vibe in the car—which had been a good vibe—changed completely and became a very bad vibe. This was a physical fact. Somehow the actual molecules in the car underwent a chemical change. The car was not the same place it had been a minute earlier. And the sky had grown darker— that was another factor.

We soon came to the facilities which had unmistakably been designed with detention in mind. Both places—there were two of them, one on the right and one on the left—were set back from the road, surrounded by high walls of razor wire, and brightly lit by arc lights. There were no windows. In the intensity and single-mindedness of their desire to contain menace they exuded it. At the same time, both places had something of the quality of IKEA outlets. I wished they were IKEA outlets. It would have been so nice if our hitchhiker had said that he had come to buy a sofa or some kitchen units and that his car had broken down. We could have sympathised with that. As it was, no one said anything. No one said anything, but I know what I was thinking: I was thinking that I had never been in a position where

I so wished I could wind back the clock just one or two minutes. I would have loved to wind back the clock, to say to Jessica, 'Shall we pick him up?' and heard her reply, 'No, let's not,' and sped past, leaving him where he was. But you cannot wind the clock back in this life, not even by two seconds. Everything that has happened stays happened. Everything has consequences. As a consequence, we couldn't have not picked him up, but I could have asked him to get out. I could have said, 'Look, man, I'm sorry, but in the circumstances would you mind getting the fuck out of our car?' I could have done this but I didn't, for several reasons. First, I was worried that if I did suggest he get out he might go berserk, might kill us. Second, I was worried that by asking—by telling him, really—to get out I would be being rude. So instead of asking him to get out we drove on in tense silence. The car sped along. There seemed no point slowing down. In any situation there is always something positive to emphasise. In this one it was the fact that there were no traffic hold-ups at all. Jessica was gripping the wheel. No one was speaking. The silence was unendurable but impossible to break. Unsure what to do, I turned on the radio. We were still tuned to a classic rock station that we had been listening to earlier in the day, before we got to White Sands, and as soon as the radio came on, in the fading light of New Mexico, I recognized the piano tinkle and swish of 'Riders on the Storm.' I am a big fan of the Doors but I did not want to hear this song now. It was unbelievable. A few moments later we heard Jim Morrison crooning:

There's a killer on the road
His brain is squirming like a toad. . . .

Having turned on the radio with such disastrously appropriate results it seemed impossible, now, to turn it off. The three of us sat there, listening:

If you give this man a ride, sweet family will die. . . .

Jessica followed the advice offered by Jim Morrison elsewhere in his oeuvre. She was keeping her eyes on the road and her hands upon the wheel. I kept my eyes on the road and my hands in my lap. Day was still turning to night. The lights of oncoming cars were dazzling and did not augur well. The song continued. Ray Manzarek was doing his little jazzy solo on the electric piano or whatever it was. We are in a totally nightmarish situation, I thought to myself. The rain on the record made it seem like it was raining here as well, under the clear skies of New Mexico, south of Alamogordo, heading towards El Paso. Before I could pursue this thought the guy in the back seat cleared his throat. In the tense atmosphere of the car the sound was like the blast of a gun going off.

'Listen, man,' he said.

'Yes?' I said. Jessica had said 'Yes?' too, at exactly the same time, and the sound of that double-barrelled query erupted into the car in a volley of desperate good manners.

'Lemme explain.'

An explanation was so precisely what we wanted. In the circumstances the only thing we could have wanted more was an unsolicited offer to get out of our car and turn himself in to the authorities.

I caught his eyes in the mirror. You often see this in films: the eyes of the person in the car framed by the rearview mirror, which is framed, in turn, by the windshield, which is framed, in turn, by the cinema screen. Basically, the look in those eyes is never benign. It is always heavy with foreboding. I met his eyes. Our eyes met. Because of all these associations it was impossible to read the look in his eyes. Also, I had recently seen an exhibition of photographs by Taryn Simon called *The Innocents*. The pictures were of men and women—usually black—who had been convicted of terrible crimes. Some of them had served twenty years of their unbelievably long sentences (hundreds and hundreds of years in some cases) but then, having won the right to DNA testing, they'd had their convictions overturned. It was not just that there was an element of doubt or that the conviction was questionable due to some procedural technicality (cops falsifying evidence of a crime which they *knew* the suspect was guilty of but could not quite prove). No, there was simply no way they could have done the terrible things for which they had been convicted. Looking at these faces, you try to deduce innocence or guilt, but it is impossible. Innocent people can look guilty and guilty people can look innocent. Anyone can look like anything. Innocent or guilty: from the faces it is impossible to judge. But while it is terrible that they were convicted of these terrible crimes, these crimes were committed by *someone*. It is even possible that the reason some of these people had been wrongly convicted was that these crimes—these terrible crimes—had been committed by the person in the back of our car, who, speaking slowly, said:

'Guess that sign freaked you out, huh?'

'That is putting it mildly,' I said. 'Also, frankly, that song did not exactly set our minds at ease.'

'Well, let me tell you what happened.'

'That would be great,' I said. I sometimes think that this is all any of us really want from our time on earth: an explanation. Set the record straight. Come clean. Let us know where we stand so that we can make well-informed decisions about how to proceed.

'I did some things in my past. I been to jail. I did some time. You hear what I'm saying? I got out more'n a year ago. But now I'm just hitching, trying to get to where I need to be. I tell you, brother, I just want to get to El Paso.'

'Well, in the circumstances,' I said. I cleared my throat. It was one of those situations in which no one could speak without first clearing their throat. 'In the circumstances I think it would be better all round if we could just drop you off.'

'Better for you. Not better for me.'

'Well, I suppose that's true but, in the circumstances . . . ' As well as constantly clearing my throat I was constantly using the phrase 'In the circumstances.' In the circumstances it was inevitable. 'Well, the truth is,' I went on, 'we were hoping to have a nice relaxing ride, and now that doesn't seem at all possible. In the circumstances, in fact, it seems extremely unlikely.'

'See, here's the thing,' he said. 'I am not inclined to get out of the car.' It must be emphasised that he did not say this at all threateningly. He was simply stating his position, but it was impossible to state this particular position without conveying an element of threat. I was worried that he was the kind of person who suffered from mood swings. Violent mood swings. I suffer from them myself. But now my mood was not swinging so much as plunging or, if such a thing is possible, swinging violently *in one direction*. Jessica was gripping the wheel and keeping her eyes on the road. I was starting in some way to feel that it was predominantly her fault that we had got into this situation. If we had been on our own—I mean, if we had somehow been in this same situation (i.e., not on our own) but somehow *on our own*—I would probably have lost my temper and told her as much.

'Lemme explain a few things,' he said. Because I was worried about cricking my neck, I didn't twist around in my seat. I kept staring straight ahead into the darkness and the oncoming lights and the red tail-lights of cars in front of us. He had been in a supermarket buying things, he said. His wife had been having an affair with another guy, and this guy's brother worked in the supermarket, and one day, when he was meant to be at work but had bunked off because he had flu . . .

I was looking at the cars coming, the hypnotic blur of lights, the inky sky, wondering what time we might get to El Paso. . . .

And then, when he came back to the supermarket . . . I realized I had drifted off, lost track of the story. In truth it wasn't a very good story, or at least he wasn't a very good storyteller. He kept bringing in all this irrelevant detail. I was very interested in his story but not in the way he told it. A few minutes earlier I was worried that he might be a murderer; now I was worried that he might be a bore, but it was possible that he was a murderer and a bore. I had been feeling for several years now that I was losing the ability to concentrate, to listen to what people said, but I had never before reached such a pitch of inattentiveness at a time when it was so important—so obviously in my best interests—to concentrate. It was so important to listen, to follow his story carefully, to pay attention, but I couldn't. I wanted to, I should have, but I couldn't. I just couldn't. It is because there are people like me doing jury service, people who can't follow what other people are saying, that there are so many wrongful convictions, so many miscarriages of justice. Whatever I was meant to be thinking about and concentrating on, I thought to myself, I was always thinking about something else, and that something else was always myself and my problems. As I was thinking this I realized that his voice had fallen silent. He had come to the end of his story. The defence had rested its case.

'We need petrol,' said Jessica.

'She means gas,' I said. A few miles later we pulled into a gas station and stopped. I hate putting gas in a car, especially in America, where you have to pay first and it's all quite complicated and potentially oily. On this occasion, though, both Jessica and I wanted to put the gas in so that we would not be left alone in the car with this guy, but we could not both get out, because then he might have clambered over the seats and driven off without us. Except he could not drive off, because we needed the key to unlock the fuel cap. Except we were in America, in a rental car, and the car did not have a fuel-cap lock. I was not thinking straight, because of the hitchhiker and everything pertaining to the hitchhiker situation. Both Jessica and I got out of the car. I did the filling up. It was quite easy. I watched the numbers— dollars, gallons and gallons of gas—spinning round the gauge on the gas pump. Although it was not my main concern it was impossible not to be struck by how much cheaper petrol was in America than in England.

Then our new friend got out of the car too. He was wearing black jeans and trainers. The trainers were not black but they were quite old. Jessica got back in the car. I was pumping gas, as they say in America. He looked at me. We were the same height except he was a bit shorter. Our eyes met. When they had met before it was in the rearview mirror of the car, but now they were really meeting. In the neon of the gas station his eyes had a look that was subject to any number of interpretations. We looked at each other man to man. Black man and white man, English man and American man.

'I need to take a leak,' he said.

'Right,' I said. 'Go right ahead.' I said this in as neutral a tone as possible. I made sure my facial expression gave nothing away and then, worried that this non-expression manifested itself as a rigidity of expression which in fact gave everything away, I relaxed and smiled a bit.

'You ain't gonna up and leave me here, are you?' he said.

'Leave you here?' I said. 'No, of course not.'

'You sure about that, brother?'

'I swear,' I said. He nodded and began walking slowly to the rest rooms. He was dragging his left leg slightly. He took his time and did not look back. I watched his retreating form. As soon as he disappeared inside, I released the trigger of the fuel line, clattered it out of the side of the car and banged it back into the metal holster of the pump. It fell noisily to the ground.

'You need to push the lever back up,' said Jessica. I did that. I pushed the lever back up and settled the awkward nozzle of the fuel hose back into it.

'Quickly!' said Jessica. I twisted the cap back onto the fuel tank, but I did it too quickly and it would not go on properly. There is much truth in the old adage 'More haste, less speed.' Eventually I succeeded in getting it on and ran round the front of the car while Jessica turned the key in the ignition. The engine roared into life.

'Go! Go! Go!' I shouted as I climbed into the passenger door. Jessica pulled away calmly and quickly, without squealing the tires, and I shut the door.

We exited the gas station safely and smoothly and in seconds were out on the road. At first we were elated to have made our getaway like this. We high-fived each other. Ha ha!

'Did you like the way I said "I swear"?' I said.

'Genius!' said Jessica. We went on like this for a bit but we soon ran out of steam, because although we still felt a bit elated we were starting to feel a bit ashamed too, and then, bit by bit, the elation ebbed away.

'Your door's not shut,' Jessica said after a while.

'Yes, it is,' I said.

'No, it's not,' said Jessica. I opened the door a crack and slammed it shut, shutter than it had been shut before.

'Sorry,' I said. 'You were right.'

'Doesn't matter,' said Jessica. Then, 'Was that a really terrible thing we just did?'

'I think it might have been.'

'Do you think it was racist?'

'I think it was just kind of rude. Judgemental. Rash.'

'Think how he's going to feel when he comes out of the toilet. He'll be so let down. He'll feel we treated him so shabbily.'

We drove on. The scene was the same—cars, lights, almost darkness. We were safe, but perhaps we had always been safe. Now that we were out of danger it seemed possible that there had never been any danger.

'It's as if he were testing us,' said Jessica.

'I know. It's never a good feeling, failing a test,' I said. 'I still remember how I felt when I was seventeen and failed my driving test.'

'How did you feel?'

'I don't remember exactly,' I said. 'Not great. What about you? You probably passed first time.'

'I did,' she said, but there was no avoiding the real subject of the moment. After a pause Jessica said, 'Should we go back?'

'Perhaps we should.'

'But we won't, right?'

'Absolutely not,' I said, and we both laughed. We drove in silence for several minutes. We were no longer elated, but the vibe in the car was good again even though we were still ashamed, innocent of nothing and guilty of nothing, relieved at what we had done and full of regret about what we had done.

'You know those urban legends?' said Jessica.

'The vanishing hitchhiker?'

'Yes. There's probably an axe in the back seat.'

I twisted around to look—a bit awkward with the seatbelt. There was nothing on the back seat and nothing on the floor either, except two Coke tins and a bottle of water, all empty, and a torn map of White Sands.

'Nothing,' I said, rubbing my neck. We drove on. It was quite dark now. Night had fallen on New Mexico.

The dashboard lights glowed faintly. The fuel gauge was pointing almost to full.

'Well,' I said. 'We performed one useful service. At least we got him away from that area where it told you not to pick up hitchhikers. He should be really grateful for that.' I said this, but as I imagined him back there, coming out of the washroom and looking round the gas-station forecourt, I knew that gratitude would not be uppermost in his mind. There would have been plenty of other cars coming and going but he must have known, deep down, that the car he wanted to see and which he hoped would still be there would be long gone. I could imagine how he felt and I was glad that I was not him feeling these things and I was glad, also, that it was just the two of us again, safe and in our car, married, and speeding towards El Paso.

7

One of my mother's three sisters, Hilda, was extremely beautiful. In what seems like a Thomas Hardy story relocated to Shropshire, she met a pupil from Shrewsbury School, the improbably named Charles Bacchus. She had been intending to go into domestic service but instead, after a courtship whose details I never learned, she married Charles and moved to London. She later separated from Charles Bacchus and began a long relationship with a self-made millionaire called Charles Brown, whom she always referred to, confusingly, as CB. They led a glamorous life. Once they drove down from London to Cheltenham in CB's white Rolls-Royce, which they parked right outside our house like a temporary monument to wealth and several kinds of mobility. They were on the maiden voyage—or maiden cruise—of the QE2. Either as part of this cruise or on another trip, they went on a tour of the American Southwest. When I was in junior school Hilda sent me brochures and postcards from places like the Painted Desert, the Petrified Forest and Monument Valley. These were landscapes I had glimpsed in Westerns, but the fact that someone I knew had been to them—had proved that they were real—gave me my first sense of elsewhere: an elsewhere that seemed the opposite of everywhere and everything I knew.

Pilgrimage

I spent the first decade of the century telling anyone who would listen that I wanted to end my days in California. One of the people I said this to, in San Francisco, was quick to put me right: you don't end your days in California, he said, you *begin* them. Jessica and I began our Californian life in January 2014, but it wasn't quite the life I'd always wanted. I'd pictured us in northern California, in San Francisco, but because of Jessica's work we wound up in southern California, in Los Angeles, in Venice Beach. Life there got off to an unexpected start—to put it mildly—and we'll come back to that later, because just as stories sometimes start with endings ('my last day in China . . . ') so beginnings can sometimes make for useful ends. Here I want to tell about our weekends, especially the Sundays when we went on little pilgrimages. It's not a religious thing—we only do it on Sundays because there's less traffic and it's easier to get around—more like a hobby, something we do with our free time. And they're not pilgrimages really, just outings in the same way that, as a boy, I used to go on drives with

my mum and dad to Bourton-on-the-Water or Stow-on-
the-Wold.

The first place we went to was 316 South Kenter Avenue in Brentwood. It was cloudy when we set off from
Venice and drove past Santa Monica Airport, where avia-
tion informs much of the surrounding development and
design. There was the museum with the life-size nose of a
FedEx plane protruding ludicrously from the front, and
the Spitfire Grill with painted fighter planes and scram-
bling pilots climbing the sky-walls. People were sitting
outside, eating and drinking, getting a few down them,
as though they were in the suburbs of a town in Kent
where developers had obtained permission for a pro-
gramme of radical modernisation while incorporating
heritage ideals of the few and their—our—finest hour.
It was lunchtime, the sky was still overcast—undercast
if you were aloft, scanning the burning blue for Messer-
schmitts or Heinkels.

Just past the Spitfire a Korean girl, model-ishly skinny,
tottered across the road in three-inch heels. A cop, not
skinny at all, was leaning against his cop car, drinking
Sunday coffee. I was expecting him to watch her cross
the road from behind his shades, to lick coffee from his
lips or wipe his mouth with the back of his hand; if he
had done so I was ready to exchange an appreciative and
knowing smile with him, but he didn't pay her—or us—
any mind.

The sky started to clear, became pale blue shortly
after we'd turned left on South Bundy Drive. Jessica
was driving, constantly wiggling and lane-hopping. We
were listening to Ornette Coleman, a conscious and

deliberately antagonistic choice given our destination. It's great music, L.A. music, but it's not really driving music except in the sense that it starts to drive you hopping mad because it's frantic, wiggling music, so frantic that even some of the songs with really cool titles and beautiful melodies eventually leave you feeling frazzled. I started flicking through an iPod crammed with some of the best music ever made, unable to find anything we could bear to hear, and then turned the whole thing off as we passed Teddy's Cafe at the intersection of Pico. A woman with swollen legs was out for the count on a bench beneath an ad for the James Brown biopic, *Get on Up*. As something to notice that was OK, but for it to have made a decent photo you'd need a third element, like a plane climbing overhead—which there was, as it happened, but it would have been impossible to get it in the frame. At Wilshire, we passed the Literati Cafe, which, like the Spitfire Grill, declared its thematic hand quite openly, even though this particular theme seemed designed to limit its appeal to fewer than the few.

Bundy became South Kenter and we were suddenly there, far more quickly than expected. It was a classic L.A. scene, neither urban nor suburban—green lawns, driveways, large houses, parked cars—even if, put like that, it seems typically suburban. Brentwood. We'd been over this way once before, for a dinner at the very fancy house of a movie agent, but although we had driven up South Kenter, right past 316, we were not aware of the significance of the address and were intent only on not being late or getting lost.

We parked the car a few houses along from 316. The

sun was strong and the street deserted. The lawns of South Kenter blazed with a brightness that seemed far in excess of their square footage unless the blazingness was a direct result of the colour being contained and thereby concentrated. Probably the time was not far off when grass could be genetically modified so that as well as being the greenest and weed-free-est grass ever seen it would also stop growing after an inch and a half so you wouldn't have to mow it. This would be hailed as a breakthrough, because time that had been wasted on mowing could now be used for other things. But this extra time would turn out to be strangely worthless, and people wouldn't do much with it except the things from which mowing the lawn had provided relief—downloading music and watching episodes of *High Maintenance* or videos that had gone viral on YouTube—so after a brief honeymoon period people would go back to old-style grass growing and take out their mowers again, and although mowing the lawn would once again become a bit of a chore people would realize that they preferred this chore to the alternative and that this constituted a limited form of enlightenment. Packaged in a different tense—all those "would"s would have to go—this was an idea I could have pitched to the agent whose amazing house we had dined at a few weeks previously, but already, in the time that I had spent pitching it to myself, it seemed to have achieved the only form in which it would ever generate any interest unless I could reconceive it as a commercial for lawnmowers which, I realized almost as quickly, is exactly what it had been all along.

We walked back to 316. There it was, the house we had come to see, the pilgrimage site. A two-storey place (three if you count the two double garages at ground level) painted white. The top floor had a narrow wrap-around terrace or balcony. There were no cars in the driveway, so the building looked inhabited but unoccupied. There was a slender green bush or tree in the middle of the two garages, and a purple plant—bougainvillea?—to the right of both. It stood there, the house, and we stood in front of it. As a pilgrimage site it wasn't exactly over-run with pilgrims. Just us. There were what looked like two entrances—we could see 318, not 316—but there seemed no doubt this was the place. I'd seen a picture of the house online and had sent it to a friend in England who is interested in this kind of stuff, asking who he thought had lived here.

'Art Pepper?' he wrote back. A good guess but wrong; it was actually Teddy Adorno, who, though an accomplished pianist, was not a great jazz fan.

Adorno came to America in 1938, moving from New York to Los Angeles in November 1941 at the suggestion of his friend and colleague Max Horkheimer, who'd arrived a few months earlier. They were not alone. A wave of émigrés from Nazi Germany had settled in southern California: Thomas Mann and Lion Feuchtwanger lived in Pacific Palisades, Bertolt Brecht (who thought he'd wound up in 'tahiti in the form of a big city') in Santa Monica. . . . There were loads of them, and we'd bought a large book with a map showing where they'd all lived.

Adorno served as musical 'helper, advisor and sympathetic instructor' for Mann while he was writing *Doctor Faustus*. He played Beethoven's 32nd piano sonata (opus 111) for him, delivered a version of the lecture that appears in the book and explained the twelve-tone system supposedly 'invented' by the fictional composer Adrian Leverkühn. Naturally, this somewhat irritated the actual inventor of the twelve-tone system, Arnold Schoenberg, who lived nearby, at 116 North Rockingham Avenue, also in Brentwood. Mann hoped to smooth things over by adding a respectful postscript in a new edition but Schoenberg was still pretty pissed because, unlike Leverkühn, he wasn't insane and didn't have 'the disease [syphilis] from which this insanity stems.' This kind of squabbling and backbiting was part and parcel of life within the émigré scene—Stravinsky (who lived in West Hollywood) and Schoenberg studiously avoided one another—and is not surprising given their extraordinary proximity.* The surprising thing is that all these European super-heavyweights, the gods of high culture, had ended up here, in a place many of

*In *The Story of a Novel,* his account of the composition of *Doctor Faustus,* Mann explains how, while reading the manuscript of Adorno's *Philosophy of Modern Music,* he 'rediscovered as a long familiar element in myself, a mental alacrity for appropriating what I felt to be my own, what I felt belonged to me.' The fulsome tribute to Adorno in *The Story of a Novel* also includes a lengthy quotation from a ten-page letter in which Mann apologised as best he could for his '"scrupulously unscrupulous" borrowings from his philosophy of music.' A few pages later he admits to running a few musical ideas by Schoenberg 'behind Adorno's back, so to speak.' In July 1948, Mann asked Adorno to furnish him with a few details and dates about his life so that he could make sure he'd got everything correct in *The Story of a Novel.* Adorno replied in tones so respectful as to be almost fawning about his anticipated 'ascent to immortality by the back door.' Four months later Mann wrote to his daughter Erika, 'I have made too much of my indebtedness to Adorno.'

them took to be the embodiment of vulgarity, rampant capitalism and crass commercialism, though this didn't stop them—the composers especially—trying to gouge money out of the Hollywood studio moguls, many of whom were themselves either part of—or the children of—an earlier generation of Jewish émigrés from Europe and weren't about to let themselves get played by some hustler (Schoenberg) insisting that the actors speak their lines in the same key and pitch as the music in a score for which he wanted fifty thousand big ones—whereupon he never heard a peep from MGM again. Such setbacks notwithstanding, Schoenberg loved L.A., even if, to his wife's annoyance, tour guides pointed out Shirley Temple's house across the way while ignoring theirs.

Also unremarked by tour guides—but indicated on our map—was Horkheimer's house at 13524 D'Este Drive, Brentwood. 'In the afternoons,' Horkheimer wrote in a letter in 1942, 'I usually see Teddie to decide on the final text with him.' The text, that is, of the book they wrote together, *Dialectic of Enlightenment,* with its famous chapter on 'The Culture Industry.' Adorno was busy working on another collaborative project, *The Authoritarian Personality,* along with solo books such as *Philosophy of Modern Music*, numerous shorter pieces and radio broadcasts.

The greatest book to come out of Adorno's eight-year stay in California, however, was *Minima Moralia: Reflections from Damaged Life* (dedicated to 'Max in gratitude and promise'). When the *Guardian* asked a number of writers to choose a book that had defined a summer for them, this was the book I picked. It doesn't seem like a summer book at all, though it becomes more summery when you realize it was written in southern California. I'd bought it from Compendium, the theory capital of London, in Camden, on 13 May 1986, and I chose it for the *Guardian* feature partly because I loved it but also to advertise myself as someone who read Adorno, to distinguish myself from novelists who I guessed would choose *The Go-Between* or *Tender Is the Night* or whatever. That's part of the Adorno mystique: the author as badge, as Karl Ove Knausgaard became *the* badge author of the 2010s. When reading Adorno, you're not just reading Adorno in the way that you might read George Eliot or E. M. Forster. 'What enriched me while reading Adorno,' writes Knausgaard in *A Death in the Family*, 'lay not in what I read but the perception of myself while I was reading. I was someone who read Adorno!'

Even Roberto Calasso, who has read everyone, who is himself another badge author, was once that someone; it's just that—being Calasso—he started early and actually met Adorno when the philosopher was writing *Negative Dialectics*. Adorno was sufficiently impressed by this 'remarkable' young man to declare, 'He knows all my books, even those I haven't written yet.'

When I became that someone—someone who read Adorno—in the summer of 1986, I was so overwhelmed by what I was reading that I had to stop reading. This is perfectly normal. Thomas Mann himself wrote to Adorno that *Minima Moralia* was 'the most fascinating reading, although it is concentrated fare that can only be enjoyed in small amounts at a time.' I was going to say that I was shocked and jolted by the current coursing through every page of *Minima Moralia,* but that would understate things. Reading Adorno, you're hurled forward and taken aback by the escalating intensity of a dialectical method in which everything is constantly turning on itself in order to surge ahead again—all within a sentence or two: 'Dialectical thought is an attempt to break through the coercion of logic by its own means. But since it must use these means, it is at every moment in danger of itself acquiring a coercive character.' Every other line is a punch line. Or a counter-punch. Some are both: 'It extrapolates in order, by the over-exertion of the too-much, to master, however hopelessly, the too-little.' In the margins next to this sentence I'd scrawled an exclamation of approval—'Phwah!'—even though I wasn't sure what the opening 'It' referred to. As that 'phwah' indicates—more appropriate to a picture of the Korean model we'd seen tottering across the road by the Spitfire than to a work of philosophy—the appeal of the book was not simply cerebral. The women I hung out with back in the mid-1980s were all radical feminists. None would ever have worn high heels—they clomped around in DMs—and all were incensed by that ad campaign for lingerie, 'Underneath They're All Loveable,' and we all would have agreed with Adorno's claim that 'Glorification of the feminine character implies the humiliation of all who bear it.' Even now, when lots of the militant feminism from the 1980s seems pretty crazy, heels and make-up, which are intended to be a turn-on, do nothing for me. When we lived in London, before moving to California, we'd often go to parties where women were wearing heels, but Jessica was always wearing flats, partly because she's tall, but mainly because we never travelled anywhere by taxi and always had to be ready to sprint for a bus or tube, even though Adorno, in a passage that seems both like a Hitchcock shooting script and the reaction of a member of the audience watching the film that was made from the script, claims that 'Running in the street conveys an impression of terror . . . Once people ran from dangers that were too desperate to turn and face, and someone running after a bus unwittingly bears witness to past terror . . . Human dignity insisted on the right to walk, a rhythm not extorted from it by command or terror.'

Footwear-wise, I also liked what Adorno said about slippers, that we like being able to slip our feet into them, that they are 'monuments to the hatred of bending down,' even if this seems to apply only to those shiny Noël Coward–type slippers rather than the Chinese ones I wear (black canvas, white soles), which have to be tugged over the heel like any other shoe. There's a lot of stuff like this in *Minima Moralia*, the kind of observations you might get in fiction, minus the time-consuming mechanics of plot and story. The description of a short-order cook in a place like Teddy's Cafe, as 'a juggler with fried-eggs' is Nabokovian, though in addition to seeing the cook as a juggler Nabokov would probably have put a spin on the eggs too. I thought of this as I made a note in my notebook, and when I looked up

at the house, the pilgrimage site, it seemed Swiss somehow, and for a moment I thought I'd come to the place
where Nabokov lived, even though that was a hotel, the
Montreux Palace, not a simple house.

We walked round the corner, onto the road that
turned out to be the discreet continuation of Bundy.
I stood in front of a sign—'Not a Through Road'—
and Jessica took a picture to send to our friend back in
England who would have got the allusion to the book by
Adorno's friend Walter Benjamin. As I stood there, waiting for her to take the picture, I remembered how Klaus
Mann had reacted to news of Benjamin's suicide: '*I could
never stand him, but still . . .* ' Right behind Adorno's
house was a modernist home with some kind of copper
fronting, deep-blue walls and cactuses on a sloping desert garden by the driveway. Behind the modernist façade
it looked like the original homely-looking home was still
standing, still being lived in. The sky was as blue as can
be, though it's always risky saying that about the sky in
L.A. The sky is routinely blue, then it gets bluer still and
then goes on to achieve a bluer blue than ever seemed
possible: a blue so intense that the earlier blue might as
well have been a coloured shade of grey, which is how
this day had begun. The knowledge that England was
in the grips of a heat wave took the shine off our visit
a bit. I had begun whitening my teeth, but the various
fillings and crowns refused to whiten, so discoloured bits
of old England were still apparent and in any case the
teeth were all crooked—not like straight-down-the-line,
born-and-bred American teeth, so white and shiny as

to be semi-transparent, as if illuminated from within, something which might actually be possible a few years from now.

I knew, when I read it, that *Minima Moralia* was composed in the molten core of the century, as Germany was being laid waste by a war of its own making. I knew that it was a book about exile. I hadn't realized how deeply and explicitly it was informed by the experience of being exiled in L.A. In a typical move, Adorno views the Californian obsession with health as a kind of sickness: 'The very people who burst with proofs of exuberant vitality could easily be taken for prepared corpses, from whom the news of their not-quite-successful decease has been withheld for reasons of population policy.' Adorno even seems, at one point, to have prophetically glimpsed the early decades of the twenty-first-century future, when everyone would be covered in tattoos: 'their skin seems covered by a rash printed in regular patterns, like a camouflage of the inorganic.' The reality has far outstripped his imaginings. A few days before coming to South Kenter, on the beach at Santa Monica, we saw an otherwise rather square-looking guy—polo shirt and shorts—with the muscles of one calf laid bare, red and entirely exposed. It was only a tattoo, but done so convincingly it looked as if he had been flayed. Was this just the beginning? Would he continue until his whole body was transformed in this way, rendering the internal external?

On the Internet I came across a picture of Adorno in a bathing suit, looking not so much puny as unformed, embryonic even. Since it was the Internet I worried that it was some cleverly photoshopped thing, but, whether genuine or not, it's highly likely that Adorno looked like this. (Maybe he refused to exercise as a tacit protest against the Aryan ideal represented by all the perfectly formed athletes with 1930s haircuts in *Olympia*.) Evelyn Juers's evocation, in *House of Exile*, of 'members of the German colony . . . standing like castaways in the shade of palm trees along the promenade' is so persuasive you'd think someone like Volker Schlöndorff would have made a feature about them, starring Maximilian Schell or Bruno Ganz, with music by Schoenberg and a potential audience of about thirty people.

We stood in the shade and then walked back round to the front of the house. Nothing had changed in the brief time we'd been away: there were no cars in the drive, no indications of anyone having come or gone and no sign of any other pilgrims. I wondered if Perry Anderson, who teaches at UCLA, ever came up here, either alone or with his friend Fredric Jameson, whose book *Marxism and Form* (also bought from Compendium, on 17 May 1985) had been my introduction to Adorno and whose later book about Adorno, *Late Marxism: Adorno, or The Persistence of the Dialectic* (bought at a book sale in Iowa City for a dollar in 2012), I'd found completely unreadable, either because it was or because I was now more stupid than I had been thirty years earlier or, in a way that is not quite dialectical, neither (which might also mean both). For me Perry is the ultimate badge, the badge of badges, and I'm always on the lookout for him in L.A., had once joked to Jessica that I'd spotted him by the beach in Santa Monica, coming out of Perry's Cafe, sporting a one-to-one-scale tattoo of a corduroy jacket, but he must be too busy to do frivolous things like going to the beach or even making a pilgrimage here, to the house where Adorno used to live. To that extent Perry is like Teddy, who, in his essay 'Free Time,' wrote about how he hated hobbies. 'As far as my activities beyond the bounds of my recognized profession are concerned, I take them all, without exception, very seriously. So much so, that I should be horrified by the very idea that they had anything to do with hobbies.' One of these activities was playing music. The photograph on the back of my copy of *Minima Moralia* shows Adorno, bald and a bit of a chubster in his big black glasses and pullover, presumably navigating the catastrophic difficulties of some piece of late Beethoven or Alban Berg, not improvising on the kind of jazz tune on which he'd famously poured scorn in a quite fantastically misguided essay in *Prisms*. As for 'those who grill themselves brown in the sun merely for the sake of a sun-tan,' well, 'dozing in the blazing sunshine is not at all enjoyable, might very possibly be physically unpleasant, and certainly impoverishes the mind.'

Much of Adorno's writing conforms to our vision of the intellectual in an environment and culture to which he was absolutely unsuited: 'a stranded spiritual aristocrat,' I read somewhere, 'doomed to extinction by "the rising tide of democracy."' This is the Adorno who claimed that America had 'produced nothing but automobiles and refrigerators,' that 'every visit to the cinema leaves me, against my vigilance, stupider and worse.' (*Every* visit? Isn't that a rather stupid thing to say? There must have been a few good films to see back then. I always feel better and less stupid after seeing *Brief Encounter* or *The Maltese Falcon,* the latter starring Peter Lorre, who, in the words of David Thomson, prowls through its shadows like the 'spirit of ruined Europe.') Terry Eagleton noticed the 'bizarre blend of probing insight and patrician grousing' in *Minima Moralia;* re-reading it on site, in L.A., I too was struck by the tone of self-blinding *hauteur,* as when he claims, 'Technology is making gestures precise and brutal, and with them men.' Self-closing doors impose 'on those entering the bad manners of not looking behind' and, as a consequence, of not holding doors open for others. This technologically driven corrosion of basic courtesies proceeds in tandem with the need to slam car and refrigerator doors, actions already imbued with 'the violent, hard-hitting, unresting jerkiness of Fascist maltreatment.' The reality, these days, is that everyone is always holding doors open for everyone else or thanking someone for doing so, all the time smiling beautifully with their Hegelian teeth, so that it seems like you're living in the most courteous place on earth even if a lot of the people doing this door holding, thanking and smiling have a phone wedged between ear and shoulder and some of them are so blissed out on sun, yoga and Neville's Haze that they'd forget everything about 'Memento' (the first section of part two of *Minima Moralia*) within five minutes of reading it. Schoenberg—a keen tennis player, pictured playing Ping-Pong in our book with the map in it—could talk of being 'driven into paradise,' but Adorno often depicted his own exile in melancholy or negative terms. 'Every intellectual in emigration is, without exception, mutilated, and does well to acknowledge it to himself, if he wishes to avoid being cruelly apprised of it behind the tightly-closed doors of his self-esteem,' he writes in *Minima Moralia*.

That, in a nutshell, is the orthodox or standardised impression. Other passages do not entirely negate this but enable us to see Adorno's Californian experience in a more nuanced way. Soon after his arrival in L.A., Teddy had written to his mum and dad, 'The beauty of the landscape is without comparison so that even a hard-boiled European like me is overwhelmed.' I liked that use of 'hard-boiled,' as though he were a philosophical investigator in the mould of Sam Spade or Philip Marlowe who ends up sounding as enthusiastic as Reyner Banham: 'The view from our new house lets me think of Fiesole. . . . But the most gorgeous are the intensive colours that you cannot describe. A drive along the ocean during the sunset is one of the most extraordinary impressions that my rather nonchalant eyes have ever seen. The southern architecture and limited advertising have created a kind of *Kulturlandschaft* [cultured landscape]: one has the impression that the world here is populated by some human-like creatures and not only by gasoline stations and hot dogs.'

These were early impressions. Later, in the foreword to *Prisms,* Adorno expressed 'something of the gratitude that he cherishes for England and for the United States—the countries which enabled him to survive the era of persecution and to which he has ever since felt himself deeply bound.' Noticing how democratic forms had 'seeped into life itself,' he was charmed, as European visitors always are, by the 'inherent element of peaceableness, good naturedness and generosity' in American daily life. And while he found much in L.A. that confirmed his suspicions about the worthlessness of life here he was, inevitably, changed by it. 'It is scarcely an exaggeration to say that any contemporary consciousness that has not appropriated the American experience, even if in opposition, has something reactionary about it,' he later decided.

But there was an element of confusion here too as he and Horkheimer mistook Los Angeles for a prophetic indicator—'the most advanced point of observation,' Horkheimer deemed it—of America as a whole. 'The exiles thought they were encountering America in its purest, most prefigurative moment,' writes Mike Davis in *City of Quartz*. Unaware of the peculiarities of southern-Californian history that made it exceptional rather than representative, they 'saw Los Angeles as the crystal ball of capitalism's future.'

In *Minima Moralia*, Los Angeles is glimpsed frequently between the lines, as it were, even if this phantom L.A. bears little relation to the city of today. It's not so much that Adorno says things that are untrue; it's more that he is responding to a reality 'that reality no longer tolerates.' As with the stuff about self-closing doors, it suits

Adorno's view of the alienating effect of capitalism to discover, in a restaurant, that 'the waiter no longer knows the menu,' but it's an observation that leaves the twenty-first-century reader with only one response: Are you fucking kidding me? The defining part of the waiter's job involves reciting the day's specials in such extreme

detail that you have to be reminded of the first items the moment he or she has finished telling you about the last. Back in the days when all waiters were assumed to be aspiring actors it was as though this recitation was part of an endless audition, with the ironic twist that some who'd brought it to a pitch of perfection would actually be typecast—stuck in the role of waiter—for the rest of their working lives (an entirely different form of alienation, one akin to that described by Brecht in the first of his 'Hollywood Elegies').

Minima Moralia is not a portrait of L.A., but the city and its culture *are* there as the black backing that enables Adorno's 'reflections' to function. In a way that is entirely appropriate for the author of *Negative Dialectics*, L.A. is turned into a kind of mirror image of itself, like a photographic negative where everything light is dark, white has turned black and so on. In fact, I realize now, this would be a cool cover for a new edition of *Minima Moralia*: a spectral view of a boulevard, palm-fringed and frosty, with a black sun freezing through the grey sky.

It's appropriate as well because, notwithstanding that enthusiastic early letter to his parents, in the pages of *Minima Moralia* the one thing L.A. never seems to be is *in colour*. Adorno seems oblivious to the light of L.A., to the amazing blues, the contemporary blaze of colour. We—people in our late fifties or older—tend to remember the weather of our English childhoods as being much better than it was, because back in the 1950s and 1960s people only took pictures if there was 'enough light' and

so the memory-shaping evidence of photography suggests a permanent light- and heat-wave that has long
since receded. In southern California, by contrast, it
takes an effort to recall that the beach *always* looked as
it does now, that sky and sea were the same perfect blue
when Adorno was here, in the black-and-white years of
the Second World War, and before that even—in the
1920s, 1890s or a hundred years B.C.

Before we started going on our driving pilgrimages we
would cycle along the bike path to Santa Monica. The
bike path is clearly marked, but there are always lots of
people walking or not even walking, just dawdling and
stopping in the middle of the path to take pictures. Even
some of the cyclists have no more idea how to ride a
bike than if they'd rented a donkey for the afternoon, so
although it's one of the nicest bike paths in the world it's
also slightly irritating, since you have to ring your bell
constantly to avoid the herds of iPod zombies and THC
drongos—some of whom don't even register that the bell
is intended as a *warning*, like the slim girl in unignorable
denim cut-offs who, smiling through a fog of narcotic
bewilderment, responded, 'What a pretty bell!'—but
since one of the attractions of California is the relative
absence of aggression, it's not in anyone's interests to
start yelling, 'Get out of the fucking bike path, arsehole!'
even if that is the thought going round and round your
head like a bicycle wheel.

On Sunday afternoons, on a small area of grass near

where the original Muscle Beach was located, people gather to do a version of acrobatics. A few are doing solo somersaults and cartwheels, but most are in pairs, practising a fusion of acrobatics and yoga called 'acro' or 'acro adagio.' One person, usually a man, provides a stable but constantly changing platform for the flyer— usually a woman—and together they move through a series of more or less complex routines. Often these moves will culminate with the flyer standing, smiling and staring straight ahead, held up above the man's head. Sometimes the flyer balances on one foot—perhaps with the other leg bent up over her back—held aloft by one thickly muscled, slightly quivering arm. I'd seen pictures of this—Charles Atlas lookalikes holding up smiling blondes in swimsuits—from the forties and fifties and had assumed that it was all about the men, that the women were trophies or symbols of what was on display: i.e., the men's strength. Either I'd got that wrong or what is being practised nowadays is different in several ways. The woman is not just held aloft; she plays an active part in the man's being able to fling her into the air and sustain her weight. As much as strength it's a matter of balance and cantilevered force, of using the weight of one part of the flyer's body—its urge to succumb to gravity—to lighten another part. And whereas from photographs it seemed that the important thing was the climactic pose, it is the fluid succession of movements and rhythm that is spellbinding. Sometimes there is no stillness, just an endless succession of unfolding movements, a constant and subtle display of physical dialectics.

I wanted to know if this was indeed a recent development, and so when one of the flyers was taking a break
I asked her if, back in the fifties, when a woman's life
consisted of looking nice and cooking dinners, it was
much more of a strong-man-type thing, but she had no
knowledge of the history of what was happening here
and seemed to think that I was suggesting that the eternal role of women was to cook and smile, even if these
days they are as heavily inked as the guys. Later, at home,
I did a bit of research and saw, from the famous photographs taken by Frank J. Thomas, that women had
indeed been active participants back in the 1950s (in
some they're actually airborne), but in the immediate
aftermath of this bungled conversation, I felt awkward

about asking anyone else about the history of acro, so I just sat and watched—still feeling awkward, because it might have seemed that I was only here to gawp at flexible, tattooed chicks in Lycra.

Given the partially clothed, physical intimacy of acro, a quite careful decorum is maintained throughout. There's a lot of Californian hugging as participants greet each other, but both parties push their bottoms outwards to make sure there is no pelvic contact. And while everything being practised cries out to be incorporated into a sequence of erotic moves in the privacy of the bedroom—or on stage at some New Age equivalent of the Raymond Revuebar—the atmosphere is so politely chaste (in a relaxed and healthy way) that to mention or even notice its implied sexual potential is to coarsen what is unfolding before your eyes.

The acro-istas are all strong and supple, though the ratio of strength to suppleness subtly varies. Some are more skilled than others, and there are a number of people who have obviously been coming here for ages, who have the air not of being in charge exactly but who, if there were an election to see who should run the show, would win by an overwhelming and happy majority even if the idea of running anything is entirely anathema to the spirit of the place, which is marked by a quite wonderful inclusiveness. Anyone can join in, at any level, and everyone helps out everyone else, contributing advice and tips (a tiny adjustment, the angle of a foot or shoulder, makes the difference between stability and collapse). Often men team up together to practise things, though it always looks as if this is more difficult than a man-woman pairing. Sometimes kids will join in, their mums or dads holding them up in the air, and you can imagine when they are fifteen or sixteen the boys will be back here, because, obviously, it's the most fantastic way to meet girls (who will have come back too), completely different to how things were for me in Cheltenham, when trying to meet girls meant going to a disco, drinking a gallon of beer, only speaking to your mates and getting punched in the face on the walk home—often by one of these mates—for reasons that were never entirely clear, though beer obviously played a part. On our second visit to acro, one of the regulars helped a girl of about eight to stand on his shoulders and do a little twirl. She wobbled, fell; he caught her, lowered her gently to the ground and asked if she would mind if they could please try that once more. It was impossible to imagine anything more charming, but the really great thing was the way that the mum sat there, happy to let this stranger, muscled like Conan the Barbarian, assume responsibility for her daughter's safety and happiness.

Obviously, I can't join in. I'm as strong and supple as a pane of thin glass, I've got too many ailments—left shoulder, left elbow and left wrist, in fact the whole of the left arm—and I'm too old, but if I'd been here ten years earlier I would have joined in. I used to be able to reach up to a horizontal bar, hang there for a few seconds and then flip myself up and over it so that I'd end up either supporting myself with the bar at my waist or continue on over, so that I'd be back where I started. It's not just that I used to be able to execute this little manoeuvre; I was always looking for opportunities to do so, especially if there were women around. The last time I managed it was in Goa in 2008. If I tried a stunt like that now I'd end up in a heap, like Dick Diver on the speedboat at the end of my favourite summer book, *Tender Is the Night*. So, when we leave and unlock our bikes to cycle back home, even though the experience of watching acro is always uplifting, I often feel somewhat cast down because I can't do stuff like this anymore. I start to think how terrible it is that life is passing by so quickly, and, almost simultaneously, to think that I'm not sure I have the patience to sit through the rest of what life, with its gradually accumulating haul of ailments, injuries and infirmities, has to offer, however glorious it might be to be cycling—I can still do that—along the maddening bike path back to Venice in the ageless light.*

I wonder if Adorno watched the goings-on at Muscle Beach, if he stood with the other intellectual expats, transfixed by what a beautiful thing—*schöne Sache*—he was seeing through the muscular lenses of his spectacles: fleeting instants in which we catch a glimpse of a unified world, of a universe in which discontinuous realities are

---

*Pathetic and vain even to mention this, but the truth is that I am still able to perform this impressive, semi-gymnastic manoeuvre. A further injury—a broken toe—meant that I couldn't play tennis for six weeks, so that my troublesome left shoulder and elbow got a well-deserved rest. Fearing a complete collapse of fitness during this time, I submitted to the strength-building physio regime I'd previously baulked at and, as a result, was able to execute a somewhat flailing version of the flip on the bar. I have since refined my technique and am once again on the look-out for opportunities to demonstrate it.

nonetheless somehow implicated with each other and intertwined so that there is momentarily effected a kind of reconciliation between the realm of matter and that of spirit. That's not me, of course; it's Freddy Jameson's gloss on a passage from *Philosophy of Modern Music,* the writing of which probably meant that Teddy spent little time gawping at Muscle Beach, that he left his study at 316 South Kenter only reluctantly.

We were ready to leave in the sense that there seemed nothing else to notice when we noticed, through the window, a figure moving in the house, or in 318 at any rate. Jessica said we should knock on the door and speak to whoever it was. As we were climbing the steps, anxious that knocking on the door was somewhat intrusive, the door was opened by a young woman. Late twenties, wearing a singlet and sweat pants. She looked like she was about to go to a yoga or Pilates class even though she was only taking out the trash. We said hi, apologised for turning up like this, but she greeted us as warmly as if we had been invited for tea—and had shown up half an hour early, when she was still getting things ready. We were interested in someone who once lived here, I said. Theodor Adorno.

'The writer? The philosopher?'

'Yes, yes,' I said.

She put down the trash and asked us in. It was a large apartment, dense with furniture, not at all contemporary-looking.

'Sorry, it's a little messy,' she said. 'I'm cleaning.' It looked spotless.

'No, not at all. We apologise for disturbing you. So this is your place?'

'I'm a tenant. The landlords are, um, challenging.'

'In what way?' In the way that Adorno was challenging: the deliberately complex sentences, thought doubling back on itself and reaching forward, threatening to throttle the reader in an ever-tightening dialectical spiral? That was part of the attraction: the chance to prove that one was up to the challenge of reading Adorno, that one had earned the I've-read-Adorno badge in the way that a commando earns the green beret.

'They don't fix things.'

The door was still open; she forced it shut.

'See? It's little things like this, like the door not closing properly.'

'And the real-estate person who rented it to you, did she sell it, in the sense of rent it, to you on the basis that Adorno lived here?'

'No, she did not.'

'And was it actually next door that he lived?'

'I've lived here four years. I think there was a switch.'

She was not clear about when the house was divided in two. She thought maybe Adorno had divided it up, separating his living space from where he worked, but this seemed unlikely. That was the kind of home improvement Bert Lawrence might have undertaken, not Teddy Adorno. It was possible, she said, that the owners who lived next door at 316 might know more. We should knock on their door and ask them.

She tugged the faulty door open and picked up the

trash, leaving us to look around. There was no sign of a lurking piano, no Adorno first editions or memorabilia. It was an unlikely place for a young woman to live on her own. I would have found it a bit depressing coming back here after a night out or even after a yoga class, knowing that whenever I wanted to go out again I'd have to clamber back into the waiting car, the second home that can end up being a first home. We stepped outside as she came back, thanked her for her time and help.

'I must find out more,' she said. 'How do you spell "Adorno" again?'

I spelled it out and we said goodbye. There was no bell on the main door, the door to 316, so we had to rap on the wood assertively, like cops—'Open up!'—come to check on German-speaking aliens. There was no answer. We had knocked hard, but it seemed possible that even if people were at home, sitting in a back room or upstairs, they might not have been able to hear us. This may have been deliberate, a response to having been disturbed too often in the past by unwanted pilgrims ringing the no-longer-there bell, asking about someone who no longer lived there.

We walked back to the car while other cars zoomed noisily by. Like so many other places in L.A., this was a place people drove past in order to get to some other place. We were people like that, people who had to get to some other place. I said at the outset that our pilgrimage wasn't really a pilgrimage, especially if a pilgrimage has to be an end in itself. You can't tag on a visit to Mecca at the end of a tour of the fleshpots of the Orient, but we had arranged our trip to South Kenter so that we could have coffee with Antoine Wilson, who also lives in Brentwood. Antoine is a novelist with a sideline as 'the Slow Paparazzo,' photographing spots where movie stars have sat, stood or walked minutes after they've left. It may look like an empty street with cars and parking meters, but Laura Dern had been here a short while before. The Hungry Cat is not just a restaurant (with the exit sign in bright green neon), it's where Ben Affleck and Jennifer Garner had just finished eating. Antoine works according to a tight set of rules. He can't turn up after a friend has tipped him off about a sighting, he has to have been there and seen the celebrities himself. And he takes the picture within minutes of their having moved on.

But what if you get to places more than sixty years after the philosopher-stars have left, after Adorno and Horkheimer returned to Germany in 1949? Is a place still touched by the same kind of magic that Antoine records and creates? And isn't that magic enhanced by the way that there is no blue plaque in commemoration, that most of the people driving along South Kenter have no idea that someone called Adorno lived here—or who this Adorno was or how his name is spelled?

A few weeks prior to our pilgrimage to South Kenter Avenue I'd met an actor called Norman Lloyd at a party. He was ninety-nine, had not only played tennis with Charlie Chaplin, but *still* played tennis. I called him up the day before coming here and asked if he'd ever met Adorno. He hadn't, it turned out.

'Though I knew Brecht rather well,' he said. It would

have been nice to establish a living connection with Adorno, but perhaps just knowing who he was, that he had lived here, was sufficient to . . . To what? To make us conscious that if we had stood here seventy years earlier, when Norman was in his twenties, we might have seen Adorno coming out of the door, could have walked up and asked for his autograph or persuaded him to invite us in.

That's pretty much what happened when, on a Sunday afternoon in 1947, the fourteen-year-old Susan Sontag turned up at Thomas Mann's house at 1550 San Remo Drive in Pacific Palisades. Sontag's friend Merrill had looked up Mann's number in the phone book, called up unannounced and—to Susan's mortification—secured an invitation for tea. The young Sontag loved *The Magic Mountain*, one of those books I wish I'd read when I was in my teens, when I had more patience, instead of in my early fifties, when I found it cosmically boring before it finally became great—even if it never stopped being boring, even right at the end, when my sense of its greatness was undoubtedly informed by the knowledge that I'd soon be done with it. People say that Mann can be funny but this seems hard to credit, even if he first envisaged *The Magic Mountain* as 'a humoristic complement' to *Death in Venice* and later thought of it as 'English humoristic expansive.' If Sontag found Mann humouristic, then that might well prove that he wasn't, since her obsession with seriousness led her to eliminate any slight natural tendency she might once have had in that direction. I worry that if I quote David Sedaris people might think that I'm not serious, but he is correct when he writes that serious is not the opposite of funny; the opposite of funny is not funny. I'm always on the brink of saying or thinking that anyone without a sense of humour is stupid, and at some level I believe this, even though it's a stupid thing to say or think, since Sontag, though not humouristic, was very clever, something that was already obvious—to her—by the time she had tea with Mann in 1947.

Sontag wrote about this visit years later in 'Pilgrimage,' a piece of not-even-disguised 'fiction' published forty years after the fact in *The New Yorker,* in 1987. It's the nearest she ever got to writing something funny. Already 'a zealot of seriousness' at the time of the visit ('Listen, that's not funny,' she scolds Merrill when he tells her he's phoned the Mann household), even Sontag is taken aback by Mann's stupendous seriousness and glacial grandeur. 'I wouldn't have minded if he had talked like a book. I wanted him to talk like a book. What I was obscurely starting to mind was that (as I couldn't have put it then) he talked like a book review.'

Why 'Pilgrimage' was published as fiction is hard to say—perhaps because the events described took place so long ago they could no longer be fact-checked? Or is it in fact, despite its apparent reliability, fictive in some now unverifiable way, a work of art as defined by Adorno in his second-best-known aphorism: 'magic delivered from the lie of being truth'?

Either way, if, when all is said and done, we were sort of pilgrims at the Adorno house, then this piece of fairly reliable non-fiction is a sort of homage to Sontag's 'Pilgrimage,' even if I only became aware of its existence after we had made our pilgrimage to the Adorno house. What starts out as one thing can become something else even if nothing in it changes. Conversely, 316 South Kenter remains what it was—Adorno's house—even though it no longer is.

8

I was back in London on the day it was announced that Charlie Haden had died in Los Angeles, the city I had just come from. As a tribute, I made a sign (reminiscent, I hoped, of the banner on the cover of the first album by his Liberation Music Orchestra) and fixed it to a window in the front of our flat:

RIP Charlie Haden 1937–2014

I propped the stereo speakers in the open window too, facing outwards, filling the street with music. Anxious that what was intended as a tribute might be perceived as a civic nuisance, I kept it to three tracks: 'Lonely Woman' from The Shape of Jazz to Come, *with Haden's mournful, melodic bass intro and the country-boy whoop of delight as Coleman cries out the first blues-drenched solo. Then 'Ramblin'' (from* Change of the Century) *with the down-home, country-sounding solo, which is really a duet with drummer Billy Higgins, who keeps the whole thing kicking and tickling along. The last track was 'Taney County' from the first of the Quartet West albums, a shit-kicking and elegiac medley for solo bass: as light-footed as a teenage girl, as old and wise as her grandma—and as vast as the Missouri sky. In the course of the eight-minute solo Haden quotes from the 'Ramblin'' solo, which takes us back by looking forward to the next Quartet West album,* In Angel City. *That record came out in 1988 but the picture on the back is from thirty years earlier, when Haden was twenty-one. He's squinting in the sunlight, bare-chested, not exactly athletic-looking, with a Marine haircut and his arms around his bass. The photo has been cropped so we don't know who was with him or what was in the background. What we do know is that the future only sounded as it did because Haden's bass dug so deeply into the soil and soul of the American heartland.*

In the film Rambling Boy, *Haden reminisces about how he'd travelled to L.A., hoping to find work as a jazz musician. At Tiny Naylor's, an all-night drive-in restaurant and hang-out for musicians, he met Red Mitchell, who introduced him to pianist Hampton Hawes. This led, in turn, to his meeting—and playing with—Art Pepper. (A clue to what's missed out from his life story in this invaluable if somewhat over-respectful documentary is obvious to anyone familiar with* Raise Up Off Me *and* Straight Life, *the respective autobiographies of Hawes and Pepper.)*

As he established himself in L.A. Haden started working with Paul Bley, whose band played at the Hillcrest. On a night off, at the Haig, he heard an alto player sitting in on a Gerry Mulligan gig, playing a solo so crazy he was promptly ordered off the stage. Haden was transfixed ('the whole room lit up for me'), but the unwanted guest left too quickly for

Haden to follow him out into the night. When he started asking around about this mysterious player, the drummer from Bley's band, Lennie McBrowne, asked if the guy was playing a plastic saxophone. He was! So McBrowne brought the guy along to the Hillcrest and introduced him to Haden. His name was Ornette Coleman. After the gig, Haden went back to Ornette's place, which was so littered with music that it was hard to open the door. They played all day and all the next night. A little later he met fellow aficionados Cherry and Higgins (who had been mentored by Coleman's long-time collaborator Ed Blackwell). They began rehearsing Ornette's music together, playing at the Hillcrest (with Bley on piano) in October 1958.

So this white boy—born in Shenandoah, Iowa, raised in the Ozarks of Missouri—with country music in the marrow of his bones is suddenly at the frontier of the avant-garde. The following year the quartet will head east, to the Five Spot in New York, to unleash the shape of jazz to come. Haden will look up and see Charles Mingus, Percy Heath, Paul Chambers—the great bass players of the age—and decide that it's best if he plays with his eyes shut, so that it's just himself and the bass, himself and the music.

Tiny Naylor's, at the junction of Sunset and La Brea, was demolished in 1984. It's now an El Pollo Loco. Where was Ornette's apartment, the place he and Haden went to after their first meeting at the Hillcrest? There's no mention of the address, either in Rambling Boy *or in any of the books I've read about Ornette. (It is possible, on the other hand, to locate the place on Wilshire where Bullock's department store used to be, where Ornette supported himself by working as an elevator operator.) On the front cover of* In Angel City *there's a photo of the Hillcrest with a small sign advertising the Ornette Coleman Quartet. Not to be confused with the country club of the same name, the Hillcrest was on Washington Boulevard, a block east of La Brea. It's not just that it's no longer there. I was unable, from the information I had, to work out exactly where it used to be.*

The Ballad of Jimmy Garrison

While Adorno was living in Los Angeles, did reports or rumours reach him about something that was happening over in the south-east of town, in Watts? That another émigré, an Italian, was building a demented trio of towers in his back yard?

I saw the towers—or a picture of them at any rate—before I'd heard about them, before I knew what they were. They're in the background of the photo on Don Cherry's album *Brown Rice:* skeletal spires silhouetted against the twilight, with Cherry in the foreground, cradling his trumpet, wearing robes that seem not only pan-African but pan-astral. Taken together, the purple-blue sky, Cherry's outfit and these skyrocket towers create the impression that this may have been the site from which Sun Ra would have chosen to blast off and return to Saturn. Cherry grew up near the towers after his family moved to Watts from Oklahoma. I'm guessing that he must have known Charles Mingus, who was born in 1922—making him fourteen years Cherry's senior—before he started playing with Ornette, before Mingus came to see the Coleman Quartet at the Five Spot in New York in 1959 (keeping, I'm guessing again, a special eye on Charlie Haden, who also plays bass on *Brown Rice*). In his autobiography, *Beneath the Underdog,* Mingus remembers 'something strange and mysterious' being built near his home ('what looked like three masts, all different heights, shaped like upside-down ice cream cones') and how local rowdies would throw rocks at the crazy Italian guy who was doing this work.

We drove over there, to Watts, on a cloudy Saturday. Instead of *Brown Rice* we were listening to 'Upper Egypt & Lower Egypt,' the long, slow-to-get-going, two-part song by Pharoah Sanders on *Tauhid*. Ten minutes of random percussion and bass and plonking around that never seems like getting anywhere. Then the bass initiates a surge that is picked up by drums, electric piano and guitar in preparation for the entry of the sax—which *still* doesn't happen, which seems imminent long before Pharoah, after further waiting, eventually comes blazing through like a comet in daylight. You've been expecting it for ages and it still feels like it comes out of nowhere. Pharoah started as an R 'n' B player, and you can feel him plugging back into that before he's crying and screaming, crying like a baby who knows that's the only way he'll ever get fed, that the cry can feast on itself.

'There they are!' I called out as soon as I saw the towers.

'Well, where else would they be?' said Jessica.

'What I meant was, we have arrived at the place where they are.'

We parked. We were always parking, either parking or driving around looking for a parking place or easing out of a parking space or getting our parking ticket validated, never confident about the procedure, worried that we had parked in some place that looked like a parking space but wasn't. Often the mere fact that a parking space was available suggested that it was not a parking space: if it had been a parking space it would already have been taken and would not have existed.

The Watts Towers looked, at first, a little smaller than anticipated. Not in height—the three main ones were tall, elegant, vying with each other for altitude—but in the way they were clustered together, hemmed in. More space between them would have made them airier, less solid-looking. The cramping, I saw as soon as we got out of the car, was the product of the six-foot metal fence around the perimeter of the site. Instead of starting at ground level the towers began, visually, six feet from the ground, over the top of the fence. Aesthetically the trick was to keep people out while allowing the sky in; like this the balance—in a place that was partly a celebration of balance—had tipped away from aesthetics towards security. Maybe the weather had played a part; unusually, the sky itself was hemmed in by a band of cloud.

We walked around the perimeter, seeing for the first time the intricacy of the structures, the abundance of decoration and ornamentation. From the *Brown Rice* photo the towers seemed made austerely of metal, but each spar, strand and tendril was covered with concrete, adorned with glinting coloured crockery, green and blue glass, bits of tiles.

The only way to get in among the towers is on a guided tour. We bought tickets at the Visitors' Center— appropriately homey rather than fully corporate. The tickets, pinky purple, were like the ones you used to get at cinemas; the guy handing them over was wearing a large black T-shirt that was just about big enough for him. We showed him the Cherry album cover on Jessica's phone.

'Oh man, that's deep,' he said. He liked the picture so much he showed it to a colleague, handed the phone back and said again how deep it was. I'd never heard the word 'deep' used in this way before. Was it an old expression that had fallen out of use or a new one that I'd not come across, something specifically African American that had not yet crossed over into general usage? I liked it but couldn't imagine myself ever saying it without sounding sceptical or ironic. Adorno was deep, obviously, but if I said he was deep it would sound like a shallow response or, worse, like I was parodying a shallow response to show the depth of my own understanding.

We had ten minutes to wait before our tour began, so we went next door, to the Mingus Youth Arts Center. I loved the way this place was named after Mingus, the honouring and the legacy. How many times, in London, had I cycled, walked or taken the bus along Brixton Road, past Max Roach Park? How cool that someone had the gumption to name it after the great drummer rather than one of the English poets: Tennyson Place, Keats Street, Shelley Way—reliable signs, always, that you are entering the world of hard-to-lets and potential threat. Not that Roach's name made crossing the park to visit a friend who lived in the flats behind it appreciably nicer. Nothing ever happened, but it was always a relief to get to his place, to hear the multiple locks being turned, to see the door opening and then being shut securely behind us again so that we could give ourselves entirely to 'Speak, Brother, Speak' or 'Money Jungle.'

Something was happening to me here in L.A., something new or at least something that had been sneaking up on me that I'd only recently become conscious of. Things from my late twenties that had meant a lot to me—films I'd seen, books I'd read or music I'd listened to—kept coming back to me with a force that had been dormant for much of the intervening thirty years. Cherry had been a constant presence—because he had mutated and evolved beyond jazz into other kinds of music that I became interested in—but Ornette, Miles and some Coltrane were re-claiming me in a way that was also touched with loss: the thoroughness of their claim was somehow related to a diminution of feeling of which I had hitherto been largely unaware. There was something deathly about it.

And Mingus had meant *so* much to me, even though he was dead before I knew anything about him, unlike Cherry, Haden and Pharoah, whom I saw play several times, all of whom I spoke to, albeit only briefly. There were plenty of pictures of Mingus in the center named after him, some album covers and CD cases on display and an exhibition of artworks, but ten minutes was plenty long enough to take everything in. We walked outside again, joined the other people on our tour: ten of us, mainly Europeans, gathered in a semi-circle. Our guide, a smiling African American woman, asked what the most important rule of the visit was going to be.

'Enjoy yourself,' said a man in an already-enjoying-himself Hawaiian shirt.

'Have fun,' said Jessica, tuning in quickly to the spirit of the place. But no, the main rule was 'Do not climb on the towers.' Fair enough—you can't have people clambering all over the towers as if they're part of an adventure playground—but it was a bit of a downer in the way that prohibitions always are.

We were admitted to the towers through a locked gate so that the guide became a warder, a turnkey, a screw. In the future an invisible force field might prevent people from entering except at designated times.

In among the tendrils and arches of the towers, we listened to the story of their creator's life. The story was consistent in broad outline with the versions of Rodia's life online, though there is considerable variation as to some of the details, including his name. Sabato Rodia—who for much of his life went by the nickname Sam, whose last name is sometimes given as Rodilo—was born in 1879 or 1880 in Rivatoli, Italy, and immigrated to the States in the 1890s. He settled in Pennsylvania, where Sabato and his brother worked in the coal mines. The brother died in an accident in the mine. Sabato moved to the West Coast, married Lucia Ucci in 1902. They had three children, lived in Seattle, Oakland and

Martinez before the marriage collapsed in 1912. He then worked as a labourer in rock quarries and as a construction tiler, and lived with another woman, named Benita.

In 1921 he bought a triangular-shaped lot here at 1765 East 107th Street in Watts. The lot measured 151 by 69 by 137 feet, and Rodia, at the age of forty-two, began to transform it into his home and his lasting monument. According to some accounts, he started work on the towers to give him something to do after he quit drinking (though Mingus remembers him 'drinking that good red wine from a bottle' as he worked). He lived with a woman named Carmen, who left him in 1927. From then on he lived alone, building the towers until 1954, when he gave the property to a neighbour and moved to Martinez to live near his sister. He was seventy-five. The following year, the neighbour sold the property to a man named Joseph Montoya, who intended to open what would have been the world's most spectacularly located taco stand. These plans came to nothing, and he in turn sold the property to two film people, Nicholas King (an actor) and William Cartwright (then a student at USC, later an editor), who began the long process of ensuring the survival of the towers.

As the talk about Rodia and his work continued, we shuffled through the site, sometimes on the edges, near the boundary walls, sometimes right by the towers, with the glinting and shining bits of glass and imprints either of the tools he'd used to make them or of anything else that came to hand: cornbread moulds, rug beaters, faucet

handles. Rodia salvaged and scavenged what he could—
rebar, glass, crockery, bottle bottoms (green for 7UP or
Canada Dry, blue for milk of magnesia), junk that might
be left over when everything else of apparent value had
already been taken and used. That is the essential contrast: the scale of the undertaking and the modest means
of its construction and materials. Klara, in Don DeLillo's
Underworld, is struck by exactly this. 'She didn't know
a thing so rucked in the vernacular could have such an
epic quality.'

The towers soared overhead, sturdy, intricate, grace-
ful: science-fictiony, daft and Gaudi-esque all at once.
They were like a forest of trees, linked by concrete creep-
ers but without any umbrella or canopy of leaves. But
they were also like inverted and bejewelled corkscrews.
Or like . . . The power of the place comes, in part, from
how impossible it is to put your finger on quite what
the towers are or look like. To Klara in *Underworld* it
seems like 'an amusement park, a temple complex and
she didn't know what else. A Delhi bazaar and Italian
street feast maybe.' Whatever we come up with, a crucial
part of the experience resides in that 'what else': a suggestion of skyrocket, the masts of a triangular ship heading east but becalmed forever in the doldrums of Watts
with only wave patterns in the perimeter walls to serve
as the sea. Our guide took these nautical references as
evidence that Rodia's heart and course were set on Italy,
the land he had come from, but this was greeted with
some scepticism by a white-haired member of our group
who spoke for us all.

'How much of this is supposition?' he wanted to know.

It was all a matter of record, she insisted, could all be verified by things Rodia had said in interviews either while the towers were being built or after he'd finished, when they began to attract the attention of the world at large. By then they had become mythic, and it is the nature of the mythic that it remains true to itself while subtly adapting to the spoken or unspoken needs of those to whom it appeals, whose hopes it embodies. But the towers' adaptive capacities are also a proven *physical* fact. They bend away from the sun, our guide told us, like sunflowers in reverse. This was met with a long silence, a breathing scepticism, but then she explained that concrete does this because of thermal expansion. The fence kept people at bay; the towers leaned away from the sun, their non-denominational appeal causing myriad meanings and associations to flow towards them, unimpeded, free. *From* them too, as if they were not ship but radio masts, transmitting the sound of which they were the visual embodiment, broadcasting their location, drawing us to them.

Those earlier mentions of Mingus and Cherry were not just circumstantial: in another passage in *Underworld* the towers put DeLillo's narrator in mind of 'a kind of swirling free-souled noise, a jazz cathedral.' The improvised nature of the undertaking, of learning in the process of doing and making—of being in the grips of something without necessarily being sure what the outcome will be—seems intrinsic to it. But jazz, in essence, is communal, and by Mingus's time there was a considerable history and a large body of theory to draw on—or reject. Rodia worked alone, building his intricate and epic solo inch by inch, without the benefit of architectural theory or the support of collaborators like Dannie Richmond, Roland Kirk or (in Ornette's case) Cherry and Haden. What he most wanted from the community—which may have been the motive for buying his plot of land here in Watts—was to be left alone, to go about the business of bringing this thing into an existence that would owe nothing to anyone else, but which would end up being for everyone.

Actually, the other half of that phrase from *Underworld*—'cathedral'—is as important as the adjective 'jazz.' From certain angles, especially in photographs, the towers loom over the landscape like the shirey spires of English cathedrals in Oxford or Salisbury. But the crucial thing is that at some point the comparisons fall short, as it were, of the ramshackle magnificence of Rodia's structures. The comparisons are helpful because they emphasise the towers' defining *what-else-ness*. But let's stick with the cathedrals for a moment and see how they measure up.

Raymond Williams once spoke of how, though moved by the great English cathedrals, he saw 'the enormous weight of them on man.' He was amazed by the 'sheer material effort involved in the production of these buildings, many of them fine churches in stone which have survived from periods in which hardly anybody actually would have had a stone house.' On the one hand, it is 'perfectly clear that this was a mode of construction imposed from above.' On the other, they suggest a willingness to expend huge amounts, 'often under protest but at times of their own will, of productive labour on buildings which had nothing whatever to do with satisfying the physical urgency of survival.' The people doing this were physically exposed 'at the very time when they were building shelter for an authority which was not human, which was not of them.'

Rodia worked by day for the means of survival and continued to labour in the evenings and at weekends, working on something that had nothing to do with either necessity, survival or personal gain. He was under no external compulsion to do this and was not collecting any tithe from the community to fund his efforts; nor was he being paid. Naturally, before he worked on his towers he had to make sure he had a house, a shelter for himself. The towers that he went on to create were not designed to shelter any kind of authority. They are an expression of authority—of his authorship—and therefore of his humanity. If that—humanity!—sounds sentimental or lazy, we can go back to another passage from Williams, in his book *The Country and the City*.

About the spread, in the eighteenth century, of English country houses and the ideas of 'heritage' they incarnate, Williams is less ambiguous. Yes, such houses are invariably beautiful, but

> Think it through as labour and see how long and systematic the exploitation and seizure must have

been, to rear that many houses, on that scale. See by contrast what any ancient isolated farm, in uncounted generations of labour, has managed to become, by the efforts of any single real family, however prolonged. And then turn and look at what these other 'families,' these systematic owners, have accumulated and arrogantly declared. It isn't only that you know, looking at the land and then at the house, how much robbery and fraud there must have been, for so long, to produce that degree of disparity, that barbarous disproportion of scale. The working farms and cottages are so small beside them: what men really raise, by their own efforts or by such portion as is left to them, in the ordinary scale of human achievement. What these 'great' houses do is to break the scale, by an act of will corresponding to their real and systematic exploitation of others.

Seen in this light the houses become 'a visible stamping of power, of displayed wealth and command: a social disproportion which was meant to impress and overawe.'

To read this passage is to be moved still more deeply by Rodia's towers. First, again in contrast with the building of the cathedrals, because no tax was levied on the surrounding community. Second, because Rodia was able to produce, in his own words, 'something big' only by dint of an effort that goes so far beyond the scope of 'ordinary human achievement.' In its way it exists in the same relation to the 'ordinary' as a Beethoven sonata does to someone teaching himself basic tunes on a piano. While Williams has to urge us to view a country house and 'think it through as labour,' it is impossible to look at Rodia's towers as anything other than labour, without thinking of the extraordinary work involved in their construction. How else *could* we regard them? So, yes, in certain extraordinary circumstances, what one family— one man—can produce is not 'so small' if his hobby consumes his entire life to the extent that there is no room in it *for* a family. The towers are disproportionately large compared with the surrounding bungalows and railroad tracks, which so often serve as indicators or gauges of flatness, but they do not 'break the scale.' They are not a visible stamping of power, still less, in another of Williams's phrases, 'visible triumphs over the ruin and labour of others'; instead, they're a gift. They don't make the buildings around them shrink but have served to raise up the surrounding community—almost as if, to revert to the idea from Heidegger mentioned earlier, the towers *caused* Watts to be founded around them.

Which makes it still more of a shame that a condition of the towers being protected and conserved is that they are surrounded by that unclimbable steel fence. The great country houses were designed to be seen *and* to keep people out. Within Rodia's modest plot and its low walls, the structures were designed to be part of the community. Hence the name he inscribed in them: 'Nuestra Pueblo,' our city. The necessary fence grants the towers a special status, which their specialness explicitly rejects. The harm done by this fence does not stop there. At the same time that the fence annexes off the towers it also shrinks them, reduces their scale. They feel confined, ghetto-ised. It's a far cry from the early sixties, when, as Thom Andersen puts it in *Los Angeles Plays Itself,* 'the Watts Towers were the first world's most accessible, most user-friendly civic monument.' He illustrates his point with nutty footage shot there by Andy Warhol in 1963. It's impossible to cavort around like that now, or even to be photographed in the way that Cherry was. You cannot be photographed by the Watts Towers; you can only be photographed by the fence that surrounds the towers. Stonehenge has been similarly shrunk—very nearly destroyed—by the measures designed to protect it.

The fence is doubly frustrating since the essence of the towers is that they are *self*-contained. At a certain point, when he was quite high up, Rodia was able to work from within the safety of each of the towers, so that the thing he was building—that grew around him—also served as a safety feature. Beyond that point, as the radius of the spire tightened, he had to step outside the spiralling cage but no scaffolding was used. The towers *were*—and remain—scaffolding: a highly decorative exo-skeleton for an absent interior. They were built with simple tools, with Rodia's own hands, from basic materials—rebar, steels twisted and bent together without welding, bolts or rivets—so that the intimacy and intricacies of their construction are not concealed but laid bare. The sense is of something organic rather than planned: as if blood flowing through one of the main structural arteries will end up going though the smaller decorative radials. The hieroglyphics and patterns imprinted in the wet cement were formed by the tools used in the towers' construction: hammers, the head of a garden hose. All of which adds to the impression of self-containment. If the towers are temples, they are dedicated to their own construction. Our guide told us that the legal limit on the height was a hundred feet. That, she said, was why Rodia brought the tallest of the three spires in at ninety-nine and a half feet. She might be right, but Rodia's story is adorned with sentiment— bits and pieces of good feeling that cling to the legend like the broken bits of crockery and glass that he stuck into the cement of his towers. It is possible that the achieved height created the ceiling beyond which they were officially forbidden to grow. Freed from bureaucratic interference, they could implicitly have continued on forever, *ad astra*, in spite of the foundations being less than two feet in depth.

This was one of the reasons why, after Rodia had moved on, the city of Los Angeles condemned his construction as unsafe. Having purchased the property for three thousand dollars in 1959, Cartwright and King devoted their energies to preventing the demolition of the towers. The campaign for their preservation in the face of the city's insistence that they be torn down (before an earthquake caused them to topple over) resulted in a deal and a test. If the structures were able to withstand ten thousand pounds of pressure—the equivalent of a seventy-mile-per-hour wind—they would be allowed to stay. On 10 October 1959, cables were attached, and force was exerted and increased until, our guide explained, the cable snapped. When a new and stronger cable was found, either the crane to which it was attached broke or the truck doing the tugging tilted on the axis of its wheels. We were getting into a realm of variant specificity where the facts are adorned so decoratively as to acquire a suggestion of the miraculous. This is either the enemy of truth or the product of insufficient documentation. It is also a highly malleable proof.

A different kind of test of their ability to withstand potential damage came in August 1965, a few weeks after Rodia had died. During the Watts riots, when the neighbourhood was set ablaze, the towers remained untouched and unmarked. This is factually correct, but Rodia didn't just leave Watts and give the towers to a neighbour because the work was complete: he was tired of battling the city for permits and fed up with vandalism. Also, Watts had changed, had, by the early 1960s, become almost exclusively African American. In her book *Pop L.A.*, Cécile Whiting writes that Rodia 'seems to have envisaged the towers at certain times as a refuge from deteriorating conditions in Watts' and 'may have abandoned his home in 1955 because of the changing population around him.' The irony is that after the uprisings the towers—spectacularly realized symbols of immigrant dreams—became resident totems of African American cultural expression and aspiration. 'In other words, at virtually the same moment as the Watts Towers were preserved as part of the city's cultural heritage, arguments broke out over whose heritage they represented.' The malleability of the towers is such that they can surmount this perceived schism; their strength allows them to hold competing claims together like rope in a tug-of-love. Within a year of the uprising, they had become, according to a prestigious reporter for *The New York Times*—Thomas Pynchon, no less—'a dream of how things should have been.' The tense is crucial. Not *how things might or will be in the future*, but, with more than a touch of regret—even of nostalgia—'should have been.' It's almost a corollary of the way the towers are always putting one in mind of something else: whatever one says always needs qualifying. Even loyal admirers would not claim them as an unqualified masterpiece. Unless . . .

We are familiar with the idea of the work of art never being completed, only ever abandoned, but Rodia would seem to have abandoned his at the moment of completion. The moment of the towers' completion was also the moment at which he was completed *by* his life's work. In another sense, they are constantly being completed or fulfilled—by things like the Cherry album cover, by the visitors who come from all over the world, by the various festivals that take place here each year. (Explanatory panels on the fence stress the importance of the Gigli Festival held in Nola, Italy: 'The Watts Towers resemble the icons used in the festival so closely that they are considered a likely inspiration for his work.') Repairs have been needed, but the surprising durability of the original work was further enhanced and authenticated when it became apparent that, over the years, it was the *repairs* that needed repairing. The towers were more robust than the means employed to preserve them. Their capacity to create legends about themselves was self-generating and inexhaustible.

The wayward greatness of the towers—resolutely local and eccentrically universal—and the scale of Rodia's achievement were attested to by admirers such as Buckminster Fuller and Jacob Bronowski (who in the course of describing a visit to the then unfenced towers in *The Ascent of Man*, declared them to be his 'favourite monument'). Whether or not Rodia created a work of art is another question. Or at least the question 'Is it a work of art?' brings with it another: what *kind* of work of art might it be? There is the tacit belief here that 'work of art' is the ultimate proof of value and test of worth (more rigorous and demanding than the force exerted by the stress test), but one of the functions of the towers might be to resist or undermine this idea—to question the legitimacy of the question being posed. Maybe the towers are *more* than a work of art and the idea of art is not an adequate gauge by which to measure this kind of achievement.

The towers are unique, but as a phenomenon of deter-mined, self-sufficient creation on an epic scale they are neither unprecedented nor without equal. John Berger has written about one such endeavour: 'a palace pass-ing all imagination,' as the postman Ferdinand Cheval termed his creation in Hauterives, in the Department of the Drôme in France. Cheval (1836–1924) worked for thirty-three years single-handedly building and sculpting his ideal palace. 'This work is naked and without tradition,' writes Berger, 'because it is the work of a single "mad" peasant.' Viewed from Watts, however, the existence of Cheval's palace means that there might be a tradition after all, even if it's a scattered and meagre one. That Rodia was unaware of such a possibility enables us to identify one of this tradition's defining elements as a lack of consciousness of such a tradition. Another is that other instances or components of that tradition remain unknown and uncelebrated by the world at large, and therefore unpreserved (to say nothing of the large number of such projects that, in spite of their creator's best intentions, were never completed). Cheval's reasonable boast—'I have carved my own monument'—might provide an epigraph for all such lonely enterprises but, by definition, those words have to be re-conceived, re-carved and re-written every time an individual pledges himself to an undertaking of this kind. Quotation is impossible, even if the message is the same.

Although our tour had started late it finished on time, in order to prevent a knock-on effect of delays. So our visit felt squeezed, hemmed in by time as well as by the security fence. We dragged our feet, took a last few sulky photographs before being marched back to the Visitors' Center. Surprisingly, as we looked back at the towers, it was not the work of a kindred spirit such as Cheval that came to mind but one that was absolutely antitheti-

cal: a monument built by others at the command of a
ruler who sought to impose his will on eternity itself.
'Look on my works, ye Mighty, and despair!' decrees
Ozymandias in Shelley's famous poem. Time destroys
and makes nonsense of this vaulting ambition. All that
remains of the ruler's ambition are 'two vast and trunk-
less legs of stone' and a 'shattered visage' amid the lone
and level sands stretching far away. Rodia's ambition
was just 'to do something big.' It wasn't *even* an ambition as usually understood. E. M. Cioran claims that the
mole blindly burrowing his tunnel is ambitious, that
'life is a state of ambition,' but, as usually understood,
ambition always has some goal beyond the satisfactions
afforded by the task itself: acclaim, recognition, fame,
money. Contra Adorno, building the towers would seem
to have been Rodia's hobby, something he did with his
free time—albeit something he pursued with unswerv-
ing single-mindedness. That's where Adorno is wrong
about hobbies: a hobby can become the defining purpose of one's life, the thing that gives it meaning even
if—as in Rodia's case—one is obliged to spend the bulk
of the day doing something else to earn a living, to buy
that time. He did all the work himself, he said, because it
would have been too complicated—more trouble than it
was worth—to explain to someone else what he was trying to do. Possibly he didn't entirely know what he was
doing. Even his claim that 'You've got to do something,
they've never got 'em in the world,' came after the fact,
after he was done. So maybe there was something akin to
Garry Winogrand's compulsive credo—'I photograph to

find out what something will look like photographed'—
about the undertaking. He built the towers to find out
what they would look like built.

Another helpful comparison is with the temples
designed by David Best at Burning Man in Nevada.
They're similarly big but, unlike Rodia's towers or Ozymandias' monument, instead of being built to last they're
built in order to be burned at the end of each year's
week-long festival. And whereas Rodia's towers were
built single-handedly, Best's are the work of hundreds
of volunteers, all working together. But both towers and
temples are community-based, providing a focus for a
neighbourhood (in the case of Rodia) or a city (admit-
tedly a temporary one in Best's case).

So Rodia got on with it, went steadily about his work
day after day, in spite of tiredness, periods of sickness
and the never-to-be-underestimated urge to lie down
on the sofa and do nothing. My uncle built his own
house after working as a brick layer during the day—
and said it nearly killed him (before he killed himself,
many years later, in the garage of the completed house).
Perhaps a cussedness was essential in enabling Rodia to
stick at the task, in the way that some people are able to
sustain grudges over several decades. He had something
to do, and he did it until it was done. Even so, there
must have been days when Rodia had to drag his ach-
ing legs to the towers and force his heavy arms to climb
them, when it was only after working for several hours

that the friction of dull drudgery gave way to the steady rhythm of ongoing accomplishment, that he no longer had to overcome the reluctance of his own body, did not have to force himself to keep going. Or perhaps, at some point, he was so habituated to working that it didn't occur to him to do anything else. This was what he did to relax. *Travailler, ça repose*: the ideal of the artist's life embodied by Rodin. Gathering materials, doggedly lugging things up the towers, day in, day out, not stopping.

For every Cheval or Rodia there must have been hundreds of eccentrics who conceived the idea of devoting their energies to doing 'something big' before running out of time, resources, energy or will. Some got bored, fed up. Having committed themselves to doing whatever it is that keeps them off the sauce, the lure of the bottle at the end of a day—or a week or a year—of thirsty work proves irresistible and, on reflection, adequately rewarding. It doesn't even need to be 'something big.' The most modest ambitions go unfulfilled: a loft conversion, a planned extension to a house, fixing a wonky front door that doesn't close properly. The knowledge that there are things to do, tasks to be completed, is enough to keep postponing them, to give life a sense of projected purpose and improvement. Having made the long-postponed decision to go into the office just three days a week so that he can have more time to devote to his frustrated urge to play the saxophone, a solicitor discovers, in the two extra days at his disposal, that the main purpose of the musical dream was to blind him to the

THE BALLAD OF JIMMY GARRISON   199

truth of his existence and identity: that he is a solicitor through and through. (Maybe men like Rodia have to exist in a state of something like sustained desperation, to be devoid of other options, even the most common one of all: the support of a marriage, happy or otherwise. 'Those with "something to fall back on" invariably fall back on it,' writes David Mamet. 'They intended to all along. That is why they provided themselves with it. But those with no alternative see the world differently.') Or think of the person who believes he has a book in him, only to discover that the imagined book is destined to stay in him, that it will not be written, will never be completed, let alone published. Such disillusion or resignation is not the preserve of those who dream of writing *a* book. Writers are dogged constantly by the fear of not being able to do it anymore. The suspicion that each book might be their last is often what fuels their continuing productivity. Fear of future inability proves to be a powerful and immediate incentive. Along the way, however, they become conscious of the books they won't or can't write. At some point many writers will contemplate doing their own version of George Steiner's *My Unwritten Books*—though for most it will take its place among their unwritten books. Under that title there are perhaps two categories of book: those that are unstarted and those that are unfinished.

For several years I have wanted to write a book called *The Ballad of Jimmy Garrison*. It would be about Coltrane's bassist, the way he stayed with Trane after Elvin Jones and McCoy Tyner had left, after the classic quartet first expanded to a sextet (with Rashied Ali and Pharoah) and then shrank back to a quintet (with Alice Coltrane taking over from Tyner on piano). It would also, necessarily, be about Ornette Coleman (with whom Garrison and Elvin recorded *Love Call* and *New York Is Now*), about the meeting of Coleman and Haden in L.A., and about Pharoah and Albert Ayler. I loved the title of this projected book even though I knew it was never going to be a book-length project, would at best be the title piece in a volume whose subtitle—*And Other Essays*—would be an admission of failure and abandonment; a failure which turned out to be more thorough-going even than that.

In 2013, Jessica and I spent four months in Williamsburg, Brooklyn. Whenever there was any excuse—a meeting on the East Side of Midtown Manhattan, an exhibition at PS1—I took the East River Ferry, one of those rare and wonderful services that combine sightseeing for tourists with functionality for commuters.

Albert Ayler's body was found in the East River on 25 November 1970. When Don Cherry first met this man 'with sparkling eyes and a happy smile' in Copenhagen he felt himself to be in 'the presence of someone that was carrying the gift and the voice and reflection of god.' Ayler played at Coltrane's funeral service on 21 July 1967 (as did Ornette and Haden). He believed that Coltrane was the Father, Pharoah the Son, and he himself the Holy Ghost. He ended up dead in the East River. There were rumours, conspiracies, but the accepted explanation is that it was suicide.

By jazz standards Ayler was not a prolific composer, but the best of his songs are amazing concentrations of jazz history: from New Orleans marching bands to music that pointed beyond what he called 'the cosmic bebop' of Coltrane. It's easy to see—to hear—what Cherry meant when he said that Ayler's best-known composition, 'Ghosts,' 'should be our national anthem' even if it's an anthem that turns the idea of nationhood—and of anthems—inside out before tearing them to shreds and, eventually, bringing them back from the dead.

I listened to the ecstatic despair of 'Ghosts,' to 'Universal Indians' and 'Omega' on repeated trips on the East River Ferry, from Williamsburg to Thirty-fourth Street or down to the Brooklyn Bridge. The few notes I made amounted to nothing except the knowledge that it was too late, that I should have written about Ayler in 1989, that there would be no more to *The Ballad of Jimmy Garrison* than the title.

It is so difficult to know whether you are giving up on a book because it really is unwriteable or if you are just being lazy, if you have rationalised the idea of its being unwriteable because you lack the stamina to stick at it, to keep grinding it out. Even if you have been writing for a long time—*especially* if you have been writing for a long time—it is almost impossible to work through the layers of subterfuge, the self-deceptions and self-exonerations that lead you to abandon a book and to forgive yourself for having done so. Once you have made the decision to abandon ship, it requires a certain amount of will-power to persist with the abandonment, not to lapse back into sneaked looks at the manuscript, to learn to ignore the little glimmers of hope, not to gnaw away at it until the 'it' becomes that which has been abandoned, that which is still in the process of being abandoned and that which is in the exhausted process of being revived. At some point complete withdrawal is the only solution. After which, it is possible that some parts of what was abandoned and discarded can be used in an entirely different way, in the creation of something new.

There are other scenarios too. You can run out of time long before you run out of ideas or sanity. Some unwritten books are the result of unfinished lives, of premature deaths. Albert Camus had the manuscript of the novel he was working on, *The First Man*, in the car with him when he was killed at the age of forty-six. Camus had popularised the mythic figure of Sisyphus, whom, he said, we should imagine happy as he rolled his rock up the hill each day. But for anyone engaged in some kind of personal labour, Rodia is a far better model, for two related reasons. His labours were, like Camus's, the opposite of futile—and they rendered the question of happiness futile, irrelevant. (Is the word 'happy' ever part of the vocabulary of the cussed?) Each day, instead of starting from scratch, from where he had begun the previous morning, he made progress. The protagonist of Richard Flanagan's novel *The Narrow Road to the Deep North* thinks of Sisyphus as an example of 'the Greeks' idea of punishment which was to constantly fail at what you most desire.' Two of these three terms ('failure' and 'dcsirc') play no part in Rodia's work—but the task he had set himself was nothing if not punishing. The punishment was all but indistinguishable from the satisfaction and success of his endeavours. With every passing day, either the towers grew or the materials for their continued growth increased. Setbacks, false turns and dead-ends became the precondition for keeping on, for making something. Mingus recalls that Rodia was 'always changing his ideas while he worked and tearing down what he wasn't satisfied with and starting over again, so pinnacles tall as a two-storey building would rise up and disappear and rise again.' But every day some small improvement was made, because mistakes, too, are essential tools.

In a famous passage about forgiveness in *The Human Condition*, Hannah Arendt writes: 'Only through this constant mutual release from what they do can men remain agents, only by the constant willingness to change their minds and start again can they be trusted with so great a power as that to begin something new.' Was there something deeply *unforgiving* about Rodia— unforgiving, that is, towards himself—something *punishing* (that word again) about his labours? He would see the error of his ways, change his mind, start over and continue with the same old thing. Always the same thing, the one thing.

Progress was made—but so incrementally as to have been imperceptible—as each day he climbed what he had built in order to build the as yet unmade. Every day (the contrast with Sisyphus is crucial) it took a little more effort to ascend to the point where he could start work. So his purpose was perhaps similar to that of people who climb mountains. Maybe the only answer to the question of why Rodia built his monument is a negative version of Hillary's famous response about why he had climbed Everest: because it wasn't there.

9

The ancient Egyptians spent much of their lives obsessing about the afterlife. They were always embalming or being embalmed, seeking to preserve themselves, but the afterlife, it turns out, is not the one for which they were so scrupulously and painstakingly prepared—the one they imagined beginning soon after their physical death. The real afterlife would occur from the mid-nineteenth century onwards, when they were excavated from their tombs of sand. Or, better, their wombs of sand, for they were not buried by the sand so much as formed in it, like models in a mould. From the moment of their discovery they were effectively reborn in monumental, idealised form, surrounded by tourists, photographed and worshipped like gods in some perpetual present.

That's how it seems at first. But lurking beneath this is the suspicion—not unjustified considering their obsession with what would become of them after death—that the ancient Egyptians devoted themselves to leaving tantalising clues as to the nature of their civilization. To do this they must have had more than an inkling—extraordinary for a people who had not read Gibbon's Decline and Fall of the

Roman Empire, *for whom history in the modern sense still lay in the distant future—that this civilization of theirs, so replete with images of permanence, was not going to last. With astonishing accuracy, they calculated what would be likely to survive and how, from that, we would be able to extrapolate backwards to their own time. (Ozymandias, in this light, was smarter than Shelley, took the longer view and had the last laugh. The sculptor designed his monument with the lone and level sands in mind, relied on them to play their part.) The discovery of the Rosetta Stone was anything but accidental: its purpose was to be preserved, found and deciphered. This also helps to explain why, despite their immense age, all of the sculptures, headdresses, art and carvings look futuristic. Just as the crew of a space ship on a journey to a planet in the distant reaches of the solar system are kept in a state of suspended animation, the ancient Egyptians knew they would have to out-wait everything the sands could throw at them: that's why they're sitting. The smiles on the faces of the sculpted pharaohs are the product of this long wager having paid off. They seem to look, simultaneously, as if they are waiting to be discovered and as if—to their eternal delight—they have just been discovered.*

Beginning

Now, right at the end, I need to go back to the beginning of our long-anticipated Californian life. We flew from London, were upgraded to business class (I'd finally got the seat I deserved, as the Norwegian flight attendant had promised) and moved into a little bungalow in Venice in January 2014. The timing was perfect: while England was sinking beneath the waves, or the rivers at any rate, the weather here, even by the high standards of Los Angeles, was exceptionally wonderful. We quickly established a nice routine: at eight o'clock we'd go for coffee—an eight-ounce cappuccino and a twice-baked hazelnut croissant at Intelligentsia. Jessica would go to her office in nearby Culver City, and I would return and try to work. Every other afternoon, I'd cycle down to the tennis courts by the beach, play for an hour and ride home again as the sun was setting over the Pacific.

Then, only a few weeks into our new life, I bent down to push some garbage into the already stuffed bin. When I stood up half the world had disappeared. It had disappeared but it was still there, sort of. The kitchen wall was visible but it didn't seem quite right: familiar but changed, as happens in dreams. Ah, now, here was something I recognized: a strip of brown wood against the pale yellow wall. It was the frame of the mirror—I was looking into a mirror but, like a vampire, I couldn't see my reflection. The mirror had become a window, but all that could be seen in this window was the wall on the other side of the room, behind me or behind where I used to be. So where had I gone?

'Something's happened to my eye,' I called out to Jessica. She was in the bedroom, but she too had semi-disappeared. I could see half of her body, but her face had gone. I thumped myself slightly on the side of the head as if that might knock everything back into place, dislodge the opaque filter that had come between me— though even that, the idea of there *being* a me, had become less certain than usual—and the world. I was getting confused as I tried to make sense of this insubstantial world in which things were and were not.

'What's happening?' she said.

'Well, whatever it is, it's well trippy!' I said. 'Where is the . . . ? Why is the wall a door?'

I was covering up one eye and then the other, trying to eliminate variables, as one does with an electrical fault (bulb, fuse, socket . . .), trying to ascertain exactly where the problem lay, which part of my sight had gone.

'I seem to be blind in one eye, the left, but I can sort of see out of it. Where have you gone?'

'I'm here.'

'So why are you just hallway?'

Jessica has often had problems with her eyes. Ten days earlier she'd gone to the ophthalmology department of the hospital with an ulcer on her cornea. That's where we should go now, she said. We had health insurance, courtesy of her work, so she called and made an appointment. They could see us at nine-thirty. It was eight-thirty now, would take twenty minutes to get there in a taxi. Which meant there was time to do what we did every morning: go to Intelligentsia for our eight-ounce cappuccinos and twice-baked hazelnut croissants, which were not as nice as the Doughnut Plant doughnuts I'd had every day when we'd lived in New York for four months the previous autumn but which had become part of our unchangeable routine. Getting ready took longer than usual. I kept asking where the thing was, the thing that I kept my health-insurance and credit cards in, the Oyster card-holder thing. And my keys. As soon as she told me, I would ask about something else, and by then I wasn't sure whether I'd picked up my cards and my keys and I'd be wondering if I needed my passport and it would turn out that I had my keys in my hand and my credit cards in my pocket. It took ten minutes to get out of the house, during which time Jessica's patience quickly frayed. It was, she said, like dealing with a cross between a half-senile pensioner and a totally monged-out teenager.

We walked to the café. I held on to Jessica's arm. The sidewalk was the sidewalk and the road was the road. There were people and cars, brilliant sunshine, colours. We waited in line and ordered the same things we ordered every day. We ate and drank as usual, and some of the world seemed to have come back. It was more like, as my mum used to say of people with some kind of mental trouble, that I was not all there.

Our Uber arrived and we were soon speeding along Venice Boulevard. I could now see something out of my left eye but I had no peripheral vision.

At the hospital, a nurse immediately gave me drops to dilate my pupils so that the ophthalmologist could take a look inside. As a result, my vision, having improved slightly in the taxi, became distorted in both eyes. An already bright world became brighter still. The ophthalmologist did simple tests, covering up one eye at a time, waggling her fingers on each side of my head, to test my peripheral vision.

'How many fingers am I holding up?'

'Two.' I could see them on the right side. On the left side, I couldn't even see her arm. The weird thing was that the result was the same whether using my left or right eye.

Within minutes she had succeeded, where I had failed, in eliminating some potential causes. Since the problem was the same in both eyes—lack of vision on the left—the cause must lurk behind the eye, in the brain. So it was either a migraine or a stroke. This was the first time the word 'stroke' cropped up. It was a word I didn't want to hear, but it was what Yeats, in a quite different context, called the surprising word that is also exactly the right word. If I'd had my wits about me I might have joked, when my sight first went, that I'd had a stroke—

but the reality, the ophthalmologist made quickly clear, was no laughing matter. We needed to go straight down to Emergency, she said, picking up the phone to alert them to our imminent arrival. Since I was ambulatory it would be faster if we walked rather than waited for a wheelchair.

So that's what we did. We ambulated through the hospital as we had previously walked to the café, with me clinging to Jessica's arm. The difference, because of the drops, was that, besides acting like an ageing teenager on E, I now looked like one as well: my pupils were the size of dinner plates.

A nurse showed us into a curtained cubicle. I changed into one of those hospital gowns that tie up at the back, the purpose of which seems to be to enfeeble you, to reduce your capacity for independent action. To walk even a few steps risks the ignominy of exposing your bottom to the world. You are now a patient, the gown decrees, the recipient of treatment, someone to and for whom things are done. An ER doctor saw me straightaway, went through the same tests as the ophthalmologist while adding some of his own. He touched my legs and face on both sides, asked if I could feel what he was doing—I could. I could also grip hard with either hand and extend both arms and legs. I could swallow and speak perfectly. After each of these little tests the doctor said 'Good.' It wasn't just reassuring to hear this; there was also the pride you felt in school, that you still feel in the course of a tennis lesson, when you get the answer right or execute a stroke correctly: the clever-kid-in-class glow, the sense of achievement and pride that you are not such a klutz, not a complete physical and mental wreck, like that guy moaning over there, all whacked out and smashed up on a gurney. Less encouragingly, I had been downgraded from my previous ambulatory status: I was now wheeled along on my own gurney to the MRI scanner in a different building. With my pupils enormously dilated, the Californian light was so strong I had to keep my eyes screwed shut.

There was only a short wait before I was fed into the MRI scanner. The procedure was very similar—but quite different—to one I'd had a few days earlier in the *Perceptual Cell* at James Turrell's retrospective at the Los Angeles County Museum. The highlight of that exhibition, for the fortunate few who'd managed to book or cadge a slot, was to be slid horizontally and alone into an MRI-looking gizmo by two assistants in white lab coats (both female, as gorgeous as the nurses in the film of *The Diving Bell and the Butterfly*). Once sealed inside, you were bathed in soft blue light. There were two settings, and I had, naturally, opted for the strongest. The light began to pulse and change. Headphones played beatless music that encouraged complete surrender to a non-corporeal world of pure light. As the fractal geometries and strobes of colour gathered pace it became impossible to tell whether these glowing patterns and acid flashes were emanations of an external world or if they were *in* your head. Deep space or inner space? Either way it was like a glimpse of infinity. Infinity, not eternity. The experience only lasted ten minutes; it was possible to lose track of oneself but not of time. I would have liked to spend hours in there, a whole day even.

In the same length of time that I'd spent in the Turrell *Cell,* the MRI made a map of whatever had happened in my brain. I emerged from the clattering soundtrack of the scanner, clambered onto the gurney and was wheeled back to my cubicle to await the results. The doctor returned within an hour.

'I'm afraid there has been a stroke,' he said. 'An ischemic stroke.' It had occurred at the back of my brain on the right side, affecting the working of the left half of my vision. They'd need to keep me in hospital overnight for more tests. My immediate reaction—Shit, I've had a stroke—was followed immediately by a second: Thank god we have health insurance. These, in turn, were quickly followed by a third: that a series of trapdoors might be in the process of opening up beneath me. One thing leads to another, each more serious than the previous. This has happened because something else is not working correctly, and *that* is wrong because something else is faulty. To find out what that next thing is, it will be necessary to burrow more deeply into your being and discover how much if any of that—your continued being—you have left.

I was wheeled up into what looked, to my still dilated, NHS-habituated eyes, like a business-class hospital room. Jessica went back to our apartment to get various things I'd need for my stay. In the rush to get out of the house and into the café—why hadn't we thought ahead, why were we so obsessed with having our coffee and twice-baked hazelnut croissants?—I had arrived like a guest who turns up at a party empty-handed. I hadn't brought a book, because I'd be unable to read. But my regular fortnightly column for the *New Republic* was due the next day and I had left my laptop at home. The column involved looking closely at a news photograph and writing five hundred words about it. Fortunately, I'd already chosen the photograph, so, in the interludes between getting wheeled in and out of tests, I began jotting down my blurry thoughts about this remembered image on the back of an envelope. One of the intervening tests was an ultrasound of my heart and carotid artery, which would, in the words of the technician running it, 'show us where we're at.' I could hear my heart whooshing and splooshing on the monitor. I had no idea if this was how it was meant to sound, but I had absolute confidence in my cardiovascular system.

'Ten bucks says my heart's in perfect shape,' I said. But he wasn't a betting man, the technician. Which was just as well—for him—because my heart and arteries were, as I'd boasted, pumping away like there was no tomorrow. Like there was going to be no end of tomorrows—tomorrows and tomorrows—any time soon.

'Least now we know what it's not,' he said when the test was completed. We knew where we weren't at.

In the early evening I had an intravenous CAT scan and Jessica returned with my laptop. We went through a personalised, amateur series of finger-waggling tests, and it seemed my vision had continued to improve. After she left I was able to type up the notes for my column, knock them into shape and file my copy, in case, for whatever reason, I was unable to do so the next day. A good decision, it turned out, though not because of any sudden deterioration in my condition. It was such a busy night that, in the morning, I was too exhausted to think. Whenever I was about to sleep someone would come in to check my blood pressure, my pulse, my temperature, to take more blood or monitor whatever else was happening in the gates and alleys of the body. I was glad of the attention, was even pleased to see the physical therapist—it's important to get stroke victims moving again as quickly as possible—even if his skills were, in my case, entirely superfluous. All of this was really just build-up to the headline attraction: the neurologist who came by shortly before midday. He was Korean, bespectacled, a little younger than me and—I'm not sure how this came up—he had a daughter at Stanford. To be in his presence, to be the beneficiary of his training and expertise, was to marvel at how thoroughly the idea of *rude* health had been left behind. He was a reassuring advert for the efficacy of polite well-being.

All the test results so far were negative, he said. Apart from the small matter of the stroke, I was in great shape. This was as expected: I played tennis and Ping-Pong all the time, cycled everywhere, was as thin as a rake. I loved soy milk. My favourite meat was tofu.

'I even take the skin off chicken!' I told him.

We then went through the familiar round of tests, at

which, without wishing to boast, I had come to excel: hand squeezing, face stroking, finger counting and so on. I was fine, my vision was almost entirely back, I could go home as soon as the paperwork was taken care of. The discrepancy between the seriousness of what had happened—everyone at the hospital was at pains to emphasise that *any* stroke is extremely serious—and the speed of my already almost complete recovery was echoed by the contrast between the extravagance and expense of the diagnostic technology and the modesty of the cure: low-dosage aspirin. Then, as the neurologist was about to leave, in anticipation of a few test results that were not yet in, he added a pre-emptive prescription for cholesterol-reducing Lipitor.

By two o'clock I was back home. I had a terrible headache but it was a very familiar form of terrible, nothing untoward, the kind I'd had hundreds of times before, a kind of hangover from the momentous events of the previous thirty hours. I slept for a couple of hours, cycled to the beach and walked by the ocean in the late surge and swell of afternoon light.

It seemed inconceivable that I could have had a stroke. I was fifty-five, way too young, and of all of my contemporaries I would have put myself last in line for such a thing happening. I'd never had a cigarette. I drank a fair bit, less than many of my friends, and was drinking less with every year. I actively disliked all the foods that you're meant to avoid. Except doughnuts and croissants. I'd always eaten a lot of pastries, and in New York my doughnut habit had got . . . not out of control exactly, but I was doing one a day for four months. Twice a week I had a couple of eggs, lightly poached, but what did that count for in the face of the overwhelming healthiness of my diet and life?

'Well, something,' the neurologist called to tell me the following day, 'has sent your cholesterol through the roof.' Instead of twenty milligrams of Lipitor, I should double the dose to bring it down as quickly as possible. After speaking with him, I remembered that, fifteen years ago, in England, my GP had said that my cholesterol was a little high. I paid it no mind, moved to a different part of London, signed on with another doctor. As far as I could recall, my cholesterol had never been tested again. Until now. Now I'd joined the great American statin-dependent democracy of high cholesterol, was being welcomed into the community of stroke victims as featured in a clutch of nicely produced brochures.

They made depressing reading, these brochures. In a friendly way they showed people of both sexes and many races going about their fulfilling post-stroke lives. These people, regardless of their race or sex, were overwhelmingly old and white-haired, and the advice—a walk is good exercise, pruning trees in the garden can be aerobically helpful—applied to a demographic to which I did not belong. Even as I rejected the proffered kinship, however, I remembered something that had happened nine months previously. I'd been sitting in a café when my left thumb and forefinger went completely numb. It had been freezing outside, but, looking back, this numbness had nothing to do with the temperature: it was absolute. Not just numb or cold, more like dead. This only lasted a couple of minutes and I soon forgot about it. On a couple of other occasions my vision had gone sort of sparkly and bleached out, but these episodes were so fleeting that I forgot about them too. Such things, I read now, might have been transient ischemic attacks: so brief they were difficult even to register until something more extreme occurred to give them definition and meaning. Until then they had nothing in common with anything you might ever think of as stroke-related.

Back in London, I often used to bump into the writer Gilbert Adair on Portobello Road, both before his stroke (always smoking, never healthy-looking) and after, when he was, as he put it, 'sadly diminished.' I last saw him, shuffling around with a friend, struggling to remember who I was, a couple of months before he died in December 2011, aged sixty-six. Gilbert was stroke-brochure material, had led a perfect stroke-conducive life. I may have been unlucky to have had a stroke at all, but it was a stroke of luck that I'd had such a mild one. Within forty-eight hours there was almost no physical difference between how I'd felt before and how I was afterwards. I was able to play Ping-Pong on Friday and Saturday (a very good workout for the eyes, one that persuaded me there was still some slight vision loss between 10:00 p.m. and midnight in the clock-dial scheme of things). On Monday I was playing tennis again. Apart from being at increased risk of another stroke I was fine—but psychologically I was conscious that the ground could open Adair-ishly beneath my feet at any moment. Every time I got out of the bath I worried that the giddy rush of blood from—or is it to?—the head might be the bow-wave of an approaching stroke. I was scared of bending down— and I was worried, constantly, about my brain.

There had certainly been some cognitive impairment—but Jessica insisted that this had occurred *before* the stroke. I used to pride myself on my sense of direction, but that had long gone south, or maybe north or east. I had trouble concentrating, but that too had been going on for ages—I put it down to the Internet, not to my brain blowing a fuse or springing a leak. So, no, nothing had gone permanently wrong in my head, or at least nothing had gone wrong that had not been in the process of going wrong for a while—but I now regarded that head and the brain snuggled warmly inside it in a new and vulnerable way. I'd been looking forward to signing up for a Medical Marijuana card in L.A., but the prospect of smoking pot (smoking in the healthy Californian sense of vaporizing) now seemed quite dreadful. While marijuana might meliorate the symptoms of some conditions, it seemed guaranteed to send the stroke victim spinning into an epic bummer in which you fixated either on the stroke you'd just had or the one that could blow your brain apart at any moment, that might be brought on by worrying about it. That was the thing about all this: it was a brain thing, and I loved my brain and the way it had been going about its business so gamely for more than half a century. Let's say you have something wrong with your liver or heart. Terrible news. But if you're lucky, if you get another one and take the right medication, you'll be back to your old self again. But with the brain, the one you were born with either works or it goes wrong and you start sliding away from yourself. Even if a better, cleverer brain—a *brainier* brain—had been available for transplant, I wouldn't have traded in the addled one I had for anyone else's. And although the problem, we'd quickly discovered, wasn't *in* my eyes, that's where it had manifested itself—and I loved my eyes too, especially here in southern California, where half of the reason for living, possibly all of it, was to see and be seen. I loved seeing the ocean and the sunlight and the gorgeous, tanned, fat-free, screen-tested bodies as they muscled and jogged along the beach, adorned with zero-cholesterol tattoos of Maori designs and lines from *Infinite Jest*. But also there, down by the beach, were the homeless and the half-mad, men and women whose brains had been torn apart by drugs or had gradually come undone because of some undiagnosed fault in the wiring.

A week after the stroke we bought a car, a Prius that had belonged to a friend who had recently died. Almost exactly a year earlier we'd had dinner with her husband while he was in London. When he got back to L.A. his wife (who, until a few weeks previously, when she'd started to feel tired all the time, was much fitter and more energetic than him) was diagnosed with cancer. We saw them both when we visited in May; she seemed to be doing well with chemo—and then, in October, she died. Another friend, in London, had died last spring after years of cancer treatment, remission and recurrence. They were both in their forties. My parents, by contrast, had lived very long lives. My dad soldiered on till his ninetieth birthday—to the day, exactly—in spite of a diet dedicated solely to increasing the chances of a stroke, cancer or heart attack. It's a shame that he wasn't around to enjoy the exquisite comedy of his healthy-eating son having a stroke at fifty-five.

In almost every respect life continued unchanged, except that I had to cut out the twice-baked hazelnut croissants and I was often unable to play tennis because of pulled muscles, which took ages to heal—a side-effect of Lipitor or a main-effect of middle age? I didn't know, but, in keeping with the advice in the brochure, I was getting plenty of other exercise, was constantly out on my bike, in the amazing light and weather. How long would you need to live here to start taking that for granted? Longer, if you're from England, than one lifetime, even one as lengthy as my dad's.

I was ready to write off the stroke as an inexplicable happening—and so was the neurologist—a new one—whom I went to see three months later, by which time my cholesterol was down to exactly where it was supposed to be. But doctors don't like mysteries, are reluctant to surrender to the inexplicable, and he proposed referring me up to another level of expertise: still another neurologist, who specialised in strokes. What did I think of that? Well, shortly after I'd started playing Ping-Pong again I'd mentioned to a friend whose father had suffered a series of strokes that I still had what I guessed was about a 2-percent vision loss on my left-hand side.

'You want that two percent back,' he said.

'I'm English,' I said. 'Ninety-eight percent of anything always sounds good to me.' So my impulse was to say the same thing to the doctor: Forget it, let's not bother advancing to this new tier of specialism. Especially as this neurologist was based in Hollywood. I'd regained my equilibrium to the extent that my default reaction to many things—like having to schlep over to Hollywood for a hospital appointment—was 'What a bore!' But I made the appointment and schlepped over there to see this new brain guy. His name was Sanjay. He looked incredibly young to be in such a senior position, but he managed to trip me up with some simple tests. With my right hand I could run my thumb from little finger to index finger without effort or thought. The first time I tried it with my left hand I made a mess of it, couldn't get the sequence right. And the second and the third. We then went through an extended series of question-and-answer tests and looked at some of the images of my brain, including the come shot, where you could see quite clearly the explosion or blob of blood of whatever it was, the thing that could have been so much worse than it was. But the finger-and-thumb routine still concerned him, and so, in the coming weeks, I schlepped back for tests that would use million-dollar gizmos to discover why I'd failed this simplest of exercises. Sanjay seemed excited by the case—but it was unclear whether this was simply for the intellectual challenges it presented rather than for my well-being. Even if the outcome of these tests changed his assessment of the cause of the stroke, would it make any difference to the treatment? I asked. Good question, he said. It might well do, depending on the outcome of those tests.

So we kept at it, chasing the source of the problem, smoking it out as if it were Bin Laden in the Tora Bora caves. At one point it seemed that there might be an abnormality in my lungs, so I went back for a test on the lungs. If that proved positive, surgery might be necessary. But that test was negative. The trail went dead. And so, in the end, like the two neurologists before him, Sanjay called it a day, resigned himself to an intellectually frustrating verdict—shit happens, even in the brain—and I continued taking Lipitor and low-dosage aspirin.

In the immediate aftermath of the stroke, I'd often thought of the line in Tarkovsky's film *Solaris:* we never know when we're going to die, and because of that we are, at any given moment, immortal. Even now, many months later, with all of those tests behind me, with my sense of the unavoidable tedium of life fully restored, when the resolution to treat each day as a gift has been largely forgotten, it still feels good, being where I've always longed to be, perched on what Adorno called 'this remote western coast.' There's a wild sunset brewing up over the Pacific. The water is glowing turquoise, the sky is turning crazy pink, the lights of the Santa Monica Ferris wheel are starting to pulse and spin in the twilight. Life is so interesting I'd like to stick around forever, just to see what happens, how it all turns out.

10

In Luxor there is a sculpture, slightly larger than life-size, of a prim king and queen sitting with her right hand on his left shoulder. He is complete, facing straight ahead, but by some accident of time half of her chest and all of her head and left arm have been sheared off at an angle. The damage is severe, the loss irreparable, tragic.

Looked at from a different angle, from the husband's right, it seems as though her left hand (which in fact is entirely absent) is on his shoulder. Imagine a couple sitting for a formal photographic portrait—a photograph in ancient stone. In the instant when the shutter clicks she dips her head behind his back, giggling at the ridiculous rigidity of the pose they have been asked to adopt. Suddenly they are made whole again.

I assumed this effect was a transitory delusion on my part, but every time I shifted position the woman moved accordingly, reconfiguring herself and re-creating the illusion. The statue has been like this for thousands of years, but its delicacy is such that the fleetingness of a moment—a movement—has been preserved in stone. The ravages of time are caught—and reversed—in an instant. Time is alive, permanently.

Notes

6 Matisse: Quoted in David Sweetman, *Paul Gauguin: A Life* (New York: Simon & Schuster, 1995), p. 554.

9 'notorious among all': Kirk Varnedoe, 'Gauguin,' in William Rubin, ed., *'Primitivsm' in 20th Century Art*, vol. 1 (New York: Museum of Modern Art, 1984), p. 189.

13 'a bit snivelling': D. H. Lawrence, *The Letters of D. H. Lawrence*, vol. 3, ed. James T. Boulton and Andrew Robertson (Cambridge: Cambridge University Press, 1984), p. 566.

14 Pissarro's bitchy remark: Quoted in Varnedoe, 'Gauguin,' p. 186.

15 'I am down': Ibid., p. 179.

17 'something indescribably solemn': In Herschel B. Chipp, ed., *Theories of Modern Art* (Berkeley: University of California Press, 1968), p. 75.

19 'dry bread': Quoted in John Berger, *Permanent Red* (London: Writers and Readers, 1979), p. 202.

76 'the invisible is real': All quotations from De Maria are from 'The Lightning Field: Some Facts, Notes, Data, Information, Statistics, and Statements,' originally published in *Artforum*, April 1980, p. 57, reprinted in Jeffrey Kastner, ed., *Land and Environmental Art* (London: Phaidon, 1998), pp. 232–33.

76 Heidegger: Quotations are from Martin Heidegger, *Basic Writings* (Abingdon: Routledge, 2010), p. 248 and p. 107.

78 John Beardsley: Reprinted in Kastner, ed., *Land and Environmental Art*, pp. 279–80.

78 'It is only for their gods': Lewis Mumford, *The City in History* (New York: Harcourt, 1961), p. 37.

85 'no bigger than': D. H. Lawrence, 'On Coming Home,' in *Phoenix II* (Harmondsworth: Penguin, 1978), p. 255.

85 'the greatest experience': D. H. Lawrence, 'New Mexico,' in *Phoenix* (Harmondsworth: Penguin, 1978), p. 142.

88 'some places seem temporary': D. H. Lawrence, 'Taos,' in *Phoenix*, p. 100.

91 Smithson: Quotations are from 'The Spiral Jetty,' in Robert Smithson, *The Collected Writings* (Berkeley: University of California Press, 1996), pp. 145–47.

94 Coplans: Quoted by Ben Tufnell in *Land Art* (London: Tate Publishing, 2006), p. 43.

116 'or even if some eminent Victorians': Annie Dillard, 'An Expedition to the Pole,' in *Teaching a Stone to Talk* (New York: Harper Perennial, 2008), p. 35.

144 'sun was strong': Cf. Susan Sontag, 'Pilgrimage,' *New Yorker,* 21 Dec. 1987, p. 46.

145 A wave of émigrés: A map of the émigrés' homes can be found at the end of Lawrence Weschler's essay 'Paradise: The Southern Californian Idyll of Hitler's Cultural Exiles,' in the catalogue *Exiles + Émigrés* (Los Angeles: LACMA, 1997), pp. 358–59.

145 'tahiti in the form of a big city': Bertolt Brecht, *Journals 1934–1955* (New York: Routledge, 1993), p. 159.

145 'helper, advisor and sympathetic instructor': Thomas Mann, *The Story of a Novel* (New York: Knopf, 1961), p. 37.

146 'the disease [syphilis]': Schoenberg quoted in Ehrhard Bahr, *Weimar on the Pacific* (Berkeley: University of California Press, 2007), p. 265.

146 'rediscovered as a long familiar element': This and other Mann quotations in the footnote are from Mann, *The Story of a Novel*, pp. 40, 121, 123 respectively. Adorno's letter to Mann is from Theodor W. Adorno and Thomas Mann, *Correspondence 1943–1955* (Cambridge: Polity Press, 2006), p. 25. Mann's letter to Erika is quoted in David Jenemann, *Adorno in America* (Minneapolis: University of Minnesota Press, 2007), p. 168.

146 The surprising thing: An account of Schoenberg's meeting with Irving Thalberg, from Salka Viertel's memoir *The Kindness of Strangers,* is quoted in Alex Ross, *The Rest Is Noise* (New York: Farrar, Straus & Giroux, 2007), pp. 295–96.

147 'In the afternoons': Horkheimer quoted in Bahr, *Weimar on the Pacific,* p. 32.

148 'What enriched me': Karl Ove Knausgaard, *A Death in the Family* (London: Harvill Secker, 2012), p. 295.

148 'He knows all my books': Adorno quoted in interview with Calasso, *Paris Review* Web site.

148 'the most fascinating reading': Adorno and Mann, *Correspondence*, p. 73.

149 'Dialectical thought is': Theodor W. Adorno, *Minima Moralia* (London: Verso, 1978), p. 150.

149 'It extrapolates': Ibid., p. 128.

149 'Glorification of the feminine': Ibid., p. 96.

150 'Running in the street': Ibid., p. 162.

150 'monuments to the hatred': Ibid., p. 110.

150 'a juggler': Ibid., p. 117.

151 *'I could never stand him'*: Klaus Mann quoted in Evelyn Juers, *House of Exile* (London: Allen Lane, 2011), p. 289.

152 'The very people': Adorno, *Minima Moralia*, p. 59.

152 'their skin seems covered': Ibid., p. 59.

153 Juers's: Juers, *House of Exile*, p. 302.

154 'As far as my activities': Theodor W. Adorno, *The Culture Industry: Selected Essays on Mass Culture* (London: Routledge Classics, 2001), p. 188.

154 'those who grill': Ibid., p. 191.

154 'a stranded spiritual aristocrat': Irving Wohlfahrt, quoted in Martin Jay, 'Adorno in America,' *New German Critique*, Winter 1984, p. 158.

154 'produced nothing but': Adorno quoted in Richard Leppert, ed., introduction to *Adorno: Essays on Music* (Berkeley, University of California Press, 2002), p. 12.

155 'every visit to the cinema': Adorno, *Minima Moralia*, p. 25.

155 'spirit of ruined': David Thomson, *The New Biographical Dictionary of Film*, 6th ed. (New York: Knopf, 2014), p. 637.

155 'bizarre blend': Terry Eagleton, *The Ideology of the Aesthetic* (Oxford: Blackwell, 1990), p. 358.

155 'Technology is making gestures': Adorno, *Minima Moralia*, p. 40.

156 'driven into paradise': Schoenberg quoted in Bahr, *Weimar on the Pacific*, p. 268.

156 'Every intellectual': Adorno, *Minima Moralia*, p. 33.

156 'The beauty of the landscape': Adorno quoted in Bahr, *Weimar on the Pacific*, p. 31.

156 'something of the gratitude': Theodor W. Adorno, *Prisms* (Cambridge, Mass.: MIT Press, 1992), p. 8.

157 'seeped into life': Adorno quoted in Jenemann, *Adorno in America*, p. 185.

157 'It is scarcely': Adorno quoted in Jay, 'Adorno in America,' p. 161.

157 'the most advanced point': Horkheimer quoted in Mike Davis, *City of Quartz* (London: Verso, 1990), p. 53.

157 'The exiles thought': Ibid., p. 48.

157 'that reality no longer tolerates': Adorno, *Minima Moralia*, p. 126.

158 'the waiter no longer': Ibid., p. 117.

166 Freddy Jameson's gloss: 'Fleeting instants . . . ' is somewhat misquoted from Fredric Jameson, 'T. W. Adorno,' in *Marxism and Form* (Princeton: Princeton University Press, 1974), p. 8.

170 'humoristic complement': Both Mann quotes are in Herbert Lehnert and Eva Wessel, eds., *A Companion to the Works of Thomas Mann* (Rochester, N.Y.: Camden House, 2004), p. 129.

171 'a zealot of seriousness': Sontag, 'Pilgrimage,' *New Yorker*, 21 Dec. 1987, p. 54.

171 'I wouldn't have minded': Ibid., p. 48.

171 'magic delivered from': Adorno, *Minima Moralia*, p. 222.

178 'something strange': This and subsequent Mingus quotes are from *Beneath the Underdog* (Harmondsworth: Penguin, 1975), pp. 30–31.

184 'She didn't know': Don DeLillo, *Underworld* (London: Picador, 1997), p. 492.

185 'a kind of swirling': Ibid., p. 277.

186 'the enormous weight': Raymond Williams, *Politics and Letters* (London: NLB, 1979), p. 309.

186 'sheer material effort': Ibid., p. 140.

187 'perfectly clear': Ibid., p.142.

187 'Think it through': Raymond Williams, *The Country and the City* (London: Hogarth Press, 1985), pp. 105–6.

192 'seems to have envisaged': This and other Cécile Whiting quotes are from *Pop L.A.: Art and the City in the 1960s* (Berkeley: University of California Press, 2006), pp. 156, 143.

193 'a dream of how': Thomas Pynchon, 'A Journey into the Mind of Watts.' *New York Times*, June 12, 1966. http://www.nytimes.com /books/97/05/18/reviews/pynchon-watts.html.

194 'a palace passing all imagination': John Berger, 'An Ideal Palace,' in *Keeping a Rendezvous* (Cambridge: Granta, 1992), pp. 84–85.

196 'life is a state of ambition': E. M. Cioran, *The Trouble with Being Born* (London: Quartet, 1993), p. 107.

196 Winogrand's: In Peninah R. Petruck, ed., *The Camera Viewed*, vol. 2 (New York: Dutton, 1979), p. 127.

199 Mamet: *True and False* (New York: Pantheon, 1997), p. 34.

202 'the Greeks' idea': Richard Flanagan, *The Narrow Road to the Deep North* (London: Chatto & Windus, 2014), p. 384.

203 'Only through this': Hannah Arendt, *The Human Condition* (Chicago: University of Chicago Press, 1958), p. 239.

215 'I even take the skin off chicken!': Cf. Johnny Utah (Keanu Reeves) in *Point Break*.

223 'this remote western coast': Adorno and Mann, *Correspondence*, p. 10.

List of Illustrations

Photograph on the frontispiece courtesy of the author.

Acknowledgements

Parts of this book have been previously published, often in very different form.

WHERE?	WHAT?
New Yorker	'Space in Time,' 'Time in Space,' *1, 2, 3, 4*
Harper's	'Forbidden City'
Granta	'White Sands'
Observer Magazine	'Where? What? Where?'
Financial Times	'Northern Dark,'* *10*
London Review of Books	'Beginning'
New Republic	*5*

I am grateful to the editors at those magazines, especially Nicholas Trautwein, Chris Cox, Matt Weiland, Christian Lorentzen, and Ben Crair. Thanks to Ethan Nosowsky for reading the entire manuscript, and to David Ulin for help with the Los Angeles chapters. Thanks also to Dan Frank, Michiko Clark, and Betsy Sallee at Pantheon, to everyone at the Wylie Agency, and to Kimberly Burns.

*At about an eighth of its present length.

JEFF IN VENICE, DEATH IN VARANASI

In Venice, at the Biennale, a jaded, bellini-swigging journalist named Jeff Atman meets a beautiful woman and they embark on a passionate affair. In Varanasi, an unnamed journalist (who may or may not be Jeff) joins thousands of pilgrims on the banks of the holy Ganges. He intends to stay for a few days but ends up remaining for months. Their journey—as only the irrepressibly entertaining Geoff Dyer could conjure—makes for an uproarious, fiendishly inventive novel of Italy and India, longing and lust, and the prospect of neurotic enlightenment.

Fiction

THE MISSING OF THE SOMME

The Missing of the Somme is part travelogue, part meditation on remembrance—and completely, unabashedly, unlike any other book about the First World War. Through visits to battlefields and memorials, Geoff Dyer examines the way that photographs and film, poetry and prose determined—sometimes in advance of the events described—the way we would think about and remember the war. With his characteristic originality and insight, Dyer untangles and reconstructs the network of myth and memory that illuminates our understanding of, and relationship to, the Great War.

History

ALSO AVAILABLE

Another Great Day at Sea
Zona

VINTAGE BOOKS
Available wherever books are sold.
www.vintagebooks.com